Malfuzat Series:
Wise Words of Sufi Saints

The Malfuzat series is a unique genre of books that records the utterances emanating from the lips of the sage through the pen of the devoted disciple. These words of wisdom are not only a source of guidance for the initiated but will also provide inspiration and edification for the general reader.

Other books in the series:

Volume 1
Pure Gold from the Words of
Sayyidi Abd al-Aziz al-Dabbagh

Al-Dhabab al-Ibriz min Kalam
Sayyidi Abd al-Aziz al-Dabbagh

Volume 2
Morals for the Heart

Conversations of Shaykh Nizam ad-din Awliya
recorded by Amir Hasan Sijzi

Volume 3
The Teachings and Poems
of Khwaja Ghulam Farid

Selections from the Maqabis-ul-Majalis
and Diwan-e-Farid

The Teachings and Poems of
Khwaja
Ghulam Farid

Published by Beacon Books and Media Ltd
Innospace
The Shed
Chester Street
Manchester
M1 5GD
UK

www.beaconbooks.net

ISBN 978-0-9954960-9-5

© Christopher Shackle

A C.I.P. record for this book is available from the British Library.

The Teachings and Poems of

Khwaja Ghulam Farid

*Selections from the Maqabis-ul-Majalis
and Diwan-e-Farid*

Introduced and Translated by
Christopher Shackle

BB
BEACON BOOKS

CONTENTS

PREFATORY NOTE

The present volume contains revised versions of my two earlier studies *The Teachings of Khwaja Farid* (Multan: Bazm-e Saqafat, 1978) and *Fifty Poems of Khwaja Farid* (Multan: Bazm-e Saqafat, 1983). Farid's poems may be compared with those of his two greatest predecessors in Punjabi and Sindhi through my English translations of Bullhe Shah, *Sufi Poems* (Cambridge Mass. and London: Harvard University Press, 2015), and Shah Abdul Latif, *Risalo* (Cambridge Mass. and London: Harvard University Press, 2018), both published in the Murty Classical Library of India.

Besides the first volume of Rukn ud-Din's record of Khwaja Farid's teachings which is translated in this book, there is an edited version of all five volumes of the complete *Maqabis ul Majalis* translated into Urdu by the late Captain Wahid Bakhsh Sial (Lahore: Islamic Book Foundation and Bahawalpur: Sufi Foundation, 1979). The other main early sources for Khwaja Farid's life are the Urdu memoirs compiled by his disciple Mirza Muhammad Akhtar the grandson of the last Mughal emperor Bahadur Shah Zafar, which have been edited in one volume by Javed Chandio as *Khwaja Farid* (Bahawalpur: Siraiki Academy, 1999).

All reliable editions of Khwaja Farid's Siraiki poetry derive from the classic edition of the *Divan-e Farid* sponsored by the Nawab of Bahawalpur which contains a valuable Urdu commentary by Aziz ur Rahman and an extended Urdu introduction by Allama Abd ur Rashid Talut (Bahawalpur: Aziz ul Matabi Electric Press, 1944). For complete translations into English prose, see Shahzad Qaiser, *The Message of Diwan-i-Farid.* (Lahore: Suhail Academy, 2009) and *Understanding Diwan-i-Farid.* (Lahore: Suhail Academy, 2011). For Khwaja Farid's less remarkable Urdu poetry, see the edition by Siddiq Tahir, *Divan-e Khwaja Ghulam Farid (Urdu)* (Bahawalpur: Urdu Academy, 1972), which is the subject of my paper 'Urdu as a Sideline; the Poetry of Khwaja Ghulam Farid', in Christopher Shackle (ed.), *Urdu and Muslim South Asia*, pp. 79-91 (London: SOAS, 1989).

My other papers and articles on Khwaja Farid include 'The Pilgrimage and the Extension of Sacred Geography in the Poetry of Khwaja Ghulam Farid', in Attar Singh (ed.) *Socio-Cultural Impact of Islam on India*, pp. 159-170 (Chandigarh: Panjab University, 1976); 'The Shifting Sands of Love', in Francesca Orsini (ed.), *Love in South Asia: A Cultural History*, pp. 87-108 (Cambridge: Cambridge University Press, 2006); 'Ghulam Farid' with further bibliography, in *Encyclopaedia of Islam*, 3rd edition (Leiden: Brill, 2012); and 'Punjabi Sufi Poetry from

Farid to Farid', in Anshu Malhotra and Farina Mir (ed.), *Punjab Reconsidered: History, Culture, and Practice*, pp. 3-34 (New Delhi: Oxford University Press, 2012). Finally, to help distinguish Khwaja Ghulam Farid from his famous early namesake, see my article 'Farid' on Baba Farid Shakarganj in Brill's *Encyclopedia of Sikhism* (Leiden: Brill, 2017).

Christopher Shackle
January 2018

INTRODUCTION

Thanks largely to his matchless collection of mystical hymns in the local language of Siraiki, Khwaja Ghulam Farid (1845-1901), of Chacharan in the former princely state of Bahawalpur, continues to enjoy an enormous local reputation. In each area of Pakistan, in fact, there is one great figure of the literary past who has achieved the status of a patron saint and symbol of local identity; and in the Siraiki-speaking area, this figure is unquestionably Khwaja Ghulam Farid, or Khwaja Farid, as he is popularly known.

So far, only two full-length studies of Khwaja Farid have appeared both written in Urdu. The first is the lengthy introduction contributed by Allama Talut to Aziz-ur-Rahman's standard edition of the *Diwan-e-Farid* (Bahawalpur, 1944), and the second Masud Hasan Shihab's book, *Khwaja Ghulam Farid* (Bahawalpur, 1963). For the pictures which they present of the Khwaja's life and personality, both authors naturally rely heavily upon the written records left by his immediate followers. As the frequency with which they quote from it shows, a very special place among these records is occupied by the memoir of the saint compiled in Persian—even then still considered the appropriate language for such production—by his disciple, Maulavi Rukn ud-Din under the title of *Maqabis-ul-Majalis*, 'The Lessons of the Meetings'. Not only does this book appear to have been much the most extensive of such records, but it would also seem to be much the most reliable: where the primary sources conflict, it is Rukn ud-Din who is nearly always preferred by the later authors of such other works as the *Gauhar-e-Shab-e-Chiragh,* written in Urdu by Maulavi Firoz.

Both later biographers were in a position to be able to supplement their older sources by referring to living informants who had known Khwaja Farid. It is inevitably becoming increasingly unlikely, with the passing of time, that reliable fresh information will be forthcoming from such sources, even at second hand: but it is to be hoped that those who take an active interest in their greatest poet may be able to take advantage even now of the special opportunity presented by the relatively recent period of his life, and to do the best they can in this regard in the few years left while it is still possible. An interesting start in the collection of the folk-legends which have come to surround the figure of the Khwaja has been made by the inclusion of such items in the anthology of Siraiki miscellanea

Wasdian Jhokan edited by Mr. Khan Rizwani (Multan, 1971), and this line of investigation will hopefully be pursued by others also.

But it is the figure of the Khwaja himself, as directly observed by contemporaries who were close to him, that must be the focal point of interest, of equal concern with the study of his works. Here there is no substitute for the primary sources. Direct access to these sources today, however, is limited both by their language and style, and by their rarity. The present translation has therefore been undertaken to help overcome these obstacles, and so to bring before a wider public a direct picture of one of the greatest figures in the literary and spiritual past of Pakistan.

Is is clear from the references given by Allama Talut in his study of Khwaja Farid that Rukn ud-Din's *Maqabis-ul-Majalis* was compiled in at least four volumes, the last being apparently in manuscript only. It is the first volume of this work which is translated here under the title of *The Teachings and Poems of Khwaja Farid*. The original Persian version appeared as a small lithographed book of 96 pages, entitled *Isharat-i-Faridi* published in an edition of 500 copies by the Bahawal Press, Lahore, in about 1903, under the auspices of the reigning Nawab of Bahawalpur, Muhammad Bahawal Khan V (1899-1907), whose family was closely linked to that of Khwaja Farid by ties of spiritual allegiance. A copy of this first volume alone is shelved in the British Library, London, as No.14724.b.7, thus making this translation possible.

BIOGRAPHY OF KHWAJA GHULAM FARID

As its title suggests, *The Teachings of Khwaja Ghulam Farid* is not a biography of the saint in the modern sense. Rukn ud-Din does, however provide an outline account of Khwaja Farid's life on the covers of his book. This provides the basic information necessary to understand the contents of the text itself, and so deserves to be reproduced here. Most of the facts given by Rukn ud-Din about the major events in the Khwaja's life are to be accepted without question, although there is some controversy among later writers as to the exact date of his birth.

Shorn of much of the verbiage which he was compelled to cultivate by his piety and the conventions of his time, Rukn ud-Din's account of the Khwaja's life runs as follows:

> 'The Khwaja was born at an auspicious moment before sunrise on Tuesday in the last decade of the month Zil Hijja, A.H. 1261 (24.12.1845). Since the great Shaikh Farid-ud-Din Ganj-e-Shakar had also been born on a Tuesday, he was named Khwaja Ghulam Farid. An

innate saint, the marks of holiness upon his brow were apparent from his infancy, as has been testified by Pir Ashraf Muhammad Sindhi.

Khwaja Ghulam Farid was one of the greatest saints, Sufis, and spiritual leaders of his age. All Shaikhs and followers of the mystic way used to have regular recourse to him. He had a perfect grasp of all branches of knowledge, whether outward or esoteric. He met with universal praise and approval, and his saintliness was unanimously agreed. His mystical utterances are a living proof of this. No one has composed more beautiful mystical poetry than he did, as is shown by his collection of *Ghazals* and *Kafis* in 'Panjabi' (i.e. Siraiki) and Urdu, also by his teachings in Persian, recorded in the *Maqabis-ul-Majalis*. No criticism is to be levelled at either his orthodoxy or his Sufism, for he had attained the ultimate stages of both, and was peerless in his piety and devotion.

All the world used to eat from his kitchen and benefit from his charity. He was so detached from this world that he devoted all the income from his lands and estates to the cherishing of the poor, who all, without reserve, bore him total and everlasting gratitude.

An outstanding mystical expert, he adopted the doctrine of the Unity of Being, in which he was followed not only by his disciples and deputies, but by many other folk in the region as well.

The Khwaja was in his ninth year when he was orphaned by the death of his holy father, Khwaja Khuda Bakhsh. He received his formal education from several teachers: in the Holy Quran from Miyan Sadr-ud-Din and Miyan Muhammad Bakhsh Khoja; in works of poetry from Maulvi Khwaja Hafiz, Miyan Ahmad Yar Khoja, and Miyan Barkhurdar Muttaqi; and Arabic instructional books from Maulavi Qaim-ud-Din.

In A.H. 1272 (1856), on the occasion of the holy anniversary-festival at Mithankot, he took his formal vow of spiritual allegiance to his elder brother, Khwaja Fakhr-e-Jahan, and became his disciple. Under the instruction of his teacher and pir he busied himself with Sufism. Through his performance of spiritual exercises and austerities, and his practice of the disciplines of meditation, he reached the ultimate stages on the mystical way. Having been granted the tokens of deputy-ship in A.H. 1277 (1860-61), he became occupied in giving people mystical instruction.

After the death of Khwaja Fakhr-e-Jahan, he ascended the Shaikh's throne as his successor in A.H. 1288 (1871), and remained upon it for thirty years. In A.H. 1292 (1875-76) he performed the pilgrimage to Mecca and Medina, accompanied by a large retinue of disciples and attendants, having first set his mind at rest by the appointment of his son,

Khwaja Muhammad Bakhsh, as his deputy. In A.H. 1298 (1881) His Highness Nawab Sadiq Muhammad Khan IV, the tenth Nawab of Bahawalpur, became his disciple. He enjoyed vast spiritual authority, having disciples and deputies in all parts, who maintain the line of his teaching.

He died from an abscess at sunset of Thursday, 7th Rabi II, A.H. 1319 (18.8.1901), departing from this world to the next, to be joined with His Maker.'

As mentioned by Rukn ud-Din above, Khwaja Khuda Bakhsh died when Farid was a young boy of nine, leaving his functions to be exercised by his elder son, Khwaja Fakhr ud Din. It was he who thus became responsible for the education and upbringing of his younger brother. Farid received an excellent education in the classical languages and formal sciences of Islam, as well as in poetry, and soon showed his considerable intellectual gifts. He remained throughout his life an avid reader, accumulating a large library, which now sadly seems to have been dispersed or destroyed. This intellectual side of his nature is quite prominently expressed in his poetry also, and must be taken into account if many of the poems are to be properly appreciated.

At the same time, Khwaja Fakhr ud Din had naturally become the head of the dynasty on his father's death, and Khwaja Farid became his spiritual disciple. He was initiated by Khwaja Fakhr ud Din, and very many of his poems pay tribute to his devotion to his elder brother and pir, and to the quality of the mystical instruction which he received from him. Khwaja Farid was still a very young man when Khwaja Fakhr-e-Jahan died in 1871. He in turn became the head of the dynasty and ruled as Pir in his own right for thirty years until his death in 1901.

By virtue of his position he commanded great material resources, the bulk of which he directed to charitable ends. Both by his office and his personal authority and prestige he exercised a powerful and far-flung spiritual influence, which transcended the boundaries of his immediate neighbourhood. His chosen place of residence was, however, the village of Chachran, on the banks of the Indus across from Mithankot in Bahawalpur. Khwaja Farid's family were already linked with the ruling dynasty of Bahawalpur, and these links were greatly strengthened by the personal devotion of the Amir Sadiq Muhammad Khan IV (1866-1899), who was Khwaja Farid's most exalted disciple. Many anecdotes are told of his faith in the Khwaja, which still has its visible memorial in the railway line which was specially constructed as a spur from the main system out from Khanpur to Chachran.

Khwaja Farid was himself fond of travel, and journeyed widely in India. In 1875 he performed pilgrimage to the holy places in Arabia, an experience which prompted him to compose a remarkable series of poems in which his impressions are vividly recorded, and the devoutness of his faith is movingly illustrated. Nevertheless, the environment of Bahawalpur was profoundly important to him, not least because it was a Muslim princely state where the old ways continued largely unchanged, unlike the rest of the Punjab where direct British rule had been imposed in 1849. Without this protective environment, it hardly seems likely that Khwaja Farid's poetic genius would have come so easily to fruition. As the general decline of traditional genres of Muslim poetry in British Punjab shows, radical political changes soon have their cultural effects. But the relatively undisturbed atmosphere of Bahawalpur state happily permitted this last splendid flowering of the old Sufi poetry.

The local environment was also vitally important to Khwaja Farid's poetry in a more direct fashion. Much of Bahawalpur is made up of the western tracts of the great Indian desert, known locally as the Cholistan or Rohi, even more extensive in those days before the extensions of the canal system. Khwaja Farid was passionately fond of this desert environment, where he is indeed said to have spent eighteen years of his life in all. Many of his finest poems describe the beauty he experienced in the desert, particularly during its brief seasonal flowering in the months of the rains. During these long periods in the desert he naturally came into close contact with its only inhabitants, the nomadic tribes. He is known to have formed a romantic attachment with a girl from one of these tribes, and married her. She is known by the title of Haram Mai Hotan, and many of the Khwaja's most beautiful and original poems are thought to be addressed to her.

We should not look to the main text of the 'Teachings' to provide us with further biographical details of this type, except incidentally; for Rukn ud-Din was not compiling a 'Life', designed merely to inform his readers, but a record of the Khwaja's utterances, intended to provide them with instruction and edification. His book thus belongs to that well-established genre of a disciple's collection of his spiritual master's oral teachings, known as Malfuzat. Countless such collections of Malfuzat had been compiled in Persian in Muslim India since the time of such medieval classics as Hasan Ali Sijzi's *Fawaid-ul-Fuad*, and most of these follow the same formal patterns of arrangement as those adopted here by Rukn ud-Din.

THE TEACHINGS

The Khwaja's teachings are, in accordance with these formal conventions, not arranged by subject, but under the particular occasion when they were heard. In his short personal conclusion, Rukn ud-Din is careful to specify that he has only included material he had himself witnessed at first hand; and this restriction accounts for the very limited period in time which is covered by the present first volume of the *Maqabis-ul-Majalis*. The observations uttered by the Khwaja, or made by Rukn ud-Din, are recorded for each occasion of their meeting in a separate entry, called a 'Lesson' (*maqbus*), which is regularly prefaced by a conventional heading which includes the time and date of the meeting. Here, apart from the isolated Lesson 1, which relates to 1885, the Lessons only cover a period of 12 months towards the end of the Khwaja's life, from August 1893 to July 1894. The absence of record for any meetings in the months September and October 1893, or in January and May 1894, suggests that about six interrupted periods, during which Rukn ud-Din was with his director, are covered by Lessons 2 to 24.

The 24 Lessons of the book obviously differ greatly in length and in interest. At times the reader may find himself irritated by the way in which themes are so rapidly dealt with, only to be dropped in favour of some apparently unrelated topic. This conventional arrangement must, of course, be subjected to selective quotation and re-ordering to provide a biography on the modern pattern. But the consequent gain in logical coherence is inevitably achieved at the price of loss of immediacy. It is surely the unblurred vividness of the picture which Rukn ud-Din conveys of the Khwaja talking to his disciples—an image which shines through his stilted formal expressions of piety—that constitutes the most precious quality of the book. As one reads on, one begins to find that the superficially jerky manner of presentation is in fact wonderfully suited to leading the mind gradually right into the seamless world of classical Islam, as conceived by one of its last great spiritual representatives in the sub-continent: for, no matter where the next abrupt change of subject takes us, we still find ourselves within that same world, whose coherence had yet to be seriously challenged by the ideological forces of the modern age, at least in the secluded Muslim princely state of Bahawalpur in the closing years of the nineteenth century.

Subsequent changes have, of course, meant that the totally unbroken quality of this world-view is no longer completely attainable: and since the aim of a translation must be to convey the true nature of its original, this seemed a sufficient reason for not attempting any rearrangement of the text. The analytic break-down of Rukn ud-Din's material has, therefore been confined to the Table of Contents, where the topics covered in each Lesson are summarised, and to an Index of Names at the end of the book. It will, nevertheless, be appropriate to draw the reader's attention here to some of the more striking features of the 'Teachings'.

Perhaps the most obvious fact which soon emerges from the book is that, while by far the greatest part of its contents is devoted to the words of Khwaja Farid, he hardly ever talks about himself. It is true that he frequently substantiates the point which he is making by his references to his very extensive reading, but he rarely draws upon his own experiences to do so. Partial exceptions to this rule are, it should be said, provided by his references to one of the central experiences of his life, his pilgrimage in 1875-76, as when he mentions his prohibition on taking snuff to members of his party (Lesson 5), or the layout of the prayer carpets at Mecca (6). Another interesting example occurs when he mentions the British method of manufacturing ice (15), almost the only occasion when the alien rulers of India receive any reference at all, except as potential converts (9).

Far more frequently, however, the points which Khwaja wishes to make to his disciples are reinforced by stories which show the practice of former saints. It is, in fact, these stories which provide many of the most immediately enjoyable parts of the book, just as their value as instruments of instruction is shown by the ease with which they are remembered long afterwards. Most of these stories relate to Khwaja Farid's own immediate predecessors in the particular branch of the Chishti Order which descended from the eighteenth century saint, Khwaja Fakhr-ud-Din of Delhi, through his disciple and successor, Khwaja Nur Muhammad of Mahar, called 'Qibla-e-Alam'. The latter's outstanding successor was Khwaja Farid's great-grandfather, Khwaja Muhammad Aqil, often referred to as 'Sahib-ur-Rauza'. Khwaja Farid's grandfather died young, but he tells many anecdotes of his father, Khwaja Khuda Bakhs, or Mahbub-e-Ilahi, and of his own immediate predecessor and spiritual director, the elder brother whom he call Khwaja Fakhr-e-Jahan. The connexions of spiritual and physical descent between these and other frequently mentioned figures are set out diagrammatically in a Table of Relationships which immediately precedes the Index at the end of the book. The Index is followed in turn by a map which shows some of the places mentioned in connexion with these saints, especially those in the vicinity or Mithankot, the seal of Khwaja Farid's dynasty and their place of burial, and of Chacharan across the Indus in Bahawalpur, which was his own place of residence.

Further stories of a similar type—although many of these are more familiar, being drawn from books rather than family memories—are also told of the great early figures of the Khwaja's Chishti Order, stemming from its founder in India, Khwaja Muin-ud-Din of Ajmer (d.1236). These include the Khwaja's namesake, Bab Farid Ganj Shakar (d.1266) and his great disciple, Khwaja Nizam-ud-Din Auliya of Dehli (d.1325). Yet a third class of stories goes still further back in time, to the period on the great Sufi masters who lived in the Middle East, before the full incorporation of India into the world of Islam. These include Shaikh Junaid (d.910); Muhammad Ghazali (d.1111), and his brother Ahmad Ghazali (d.1126): and Abdul Qadir Gilani (d.1166). But there is no real distinction drawn between these historically different groups, since all were living members of the company of saints, the discussion of whose qualities was a subject of such immediate and enduring interest to the Khwaja and his disciples. Thus we find the Khwaja's teaching on the need to forgive those who speak ill of us illustrated first by a story of Khwaja Nizam-ud-Din, then by a parallel anecdote from the life of his own father, Khwaja Mahbub-e-Ilahi (Lesson 5): similarly, a mention of his great-grandfather's gratitude for his perfect faith follows naturally from a story illustrating Shaikh Junaid's teaching on giving thanks to God only after death (8). The stories may be separated in historical time by some 900 years, but they quite naturally exist side by side in the Khwaja's all-enclosing world-vision to which Rukn ud-Din introduces us.

The different themes which the stories of the saints serve to illustrate and support are equally varied, yet interconnected in character. We have already mentioned two pairs of stories that deal with questions of personal morality and right thinking. Such questions are naturally connected in any coherent religious world-view, but especially in that of Islam, with many other issues of belief and practice. It is thus no surprise to find the injunctions against any leanings towards Shiism, which form so prominent a part of the Khwaja's orthodoxy, supported by the story of his great-grandfather's tacit condemnation of a mildly Shiite Maulavi (20). While the Khwaja's own partial ban on the use of musicians at weddings in the same Lesson needs to be seen in the light of the earlier story about Khwaja Qibla-e-Alam's carefully reasoned reservations about interfering with such un-Islamic practices (5). Other stories in turn make the point that a strictly literal orthodoxy needs to yield second place to the greater latitude which stems from true spiritual insight: this theme is well illustrated by the mention of Khwaja Mahbub-e-Ilahi's attitude to minor irregularities of pronunciation while reciting the Arabic formulas of the prayer (18), supported by the preceding references to the teaching of the Holy Prophet on the point, and to that of the great early saint, Hasan Basri (d.728).

Whatever the particular moral to which they are pointing, an important subsidiary element in all these stories is their emphasis on the supremacy of the saints, especially those to whom one owes particular allegiance. The Khwaja shows himself well aware of the distortions to which this can lead (11), but does not hesitate to uphold the supremacy of his own dynasty over those descended from the other deputies licensed by the central figure of Khwaja Qibla-e-Alam (9). The continual talk of the relative supremacy of different deputies (Khalifa) and appointed successors (Khalifa-e-Janishin) may be found somewhat tedious by modern readers, but without an appreciation of the importance and interest which the subject of lines of true spiritual descent had for the author of the 'Teachings', it is hardly possible to understand his book. Rukn ud-Din of course loses no opportunity to magnify his own Khwaja. Just as Khwaja Farid has earlier emphasized the eminence of his spiritual ancestor, Khwaja Fakhr-ud-Din of Delhi, by talking of the total devotion to him entertained by such a royal personage as Nawab Ghazi-ud-Din Khan of the Deccan (9), so does Rukn ud-Din reverse his usual rule of not mentioning members of the Khwaja's circle by name to refer to the arrival of Nawab Dastgir Khan to pay his respects to the Khwaja at Mithankot (17), or to the receipt of a letter from the Khwaja's most munificent follower, Nawab Sadiq Muhammad Khan IV of Bahawalpur (22). The temporal pomp which a successful dynasty of saints could maintain through the generations, thanks to the devotion of its disciples, is well brought out by the discussion of the outstanding cooks attached to the Khwaja's family public kitchen (20), although it is important to remember that, as Rukn ud-Din emphasized in his Introduction which was summarised above, the poor ate from these kitchens equally with the rich.

The doctrine of the absolute supremacy of the saints could of course, lead to serious abuses, and is only to be justified by the efficacy of their teaching. The Khwaja's stories and Rukn ud-Din's observations do not allow us to doubt the doctrine that was indeed justified in the case of dynasty of Mithankot. Besides numerous tales of their miracles, we are frequently reminded of the awesome consequences to a disciple of disregarding their instructions. The marvellous set of stories about Hafiz Jan Muhammad, after he had gone mad through disobedience to his pir, constitute one of the most memorable parts of the book (9), and will perhaps convince of the need for such apparently arbitrary rules as that which forbade leaving one's Shaikh on a Wednesday, one of the Khwaja's favourite themes (13, 15, 24).

It is certainly only when the imaginative effort is made to enter into the pious, even credulous, frame of mind of a devout disciple that we can really hope to learn from this book. No doubt Rukn ud-Din was in some respects blinkered by his devotion—and his reliability can only be properly assessed by a full comparison with the other contemporary records—but he certainly allows us a remarkably full glimpse of the living figure of the Khwaja, and was therefore entirely successful in the aim which he sets out in his conclusion, of letting the saint appear directly to the reader.

One looks to such accounts as Rukn ud-Din's after all, to provide a picture of the man which will help deepen one's understanding of Khwaja Farid's poetry: and here we are richly rewarded for a little perseverance. The Khwaja's personal devotions will, of course, be accepted without the need for further proof; but Rukn ud-Din does provide interesting details of his customary private devotions (17, 20, 21), even of his lavish manner of ablution (22). His learning is amply evidenced by the number of reference to different books made during the course of the Lessons, as is the range of his interests by the mention of such varied subjects as comparative religion (8), medicine (15), cooking (20), or music (22). The claims which are made for the rationality of Khwaja Farid's outlook are well vindicated by the account of his impeccable reasoning, albeit in terms of a discredited cosmology (12): and his fortitude is demonstrated by his endurance of the June heat at Mithankot, at the hottest time of the year in one of the hottest areas of the world (14, 17). Nor would we willingly be without the more human touches which Rukn ud-Din occasionally presents as in his self-deprecatory account of the Khwaja's annoyance at his failure to report his presence (19). Even Rukn ud-Din's determined piety cannot exclude all reference to the Khawaja's humour, which comes through vividly in the story of how he twitted the musician who complained about his colleague being rewarded with an unlucky number of rupees (7), or in the nicely oblique touch where the Khwaja says of the crazy Hafiz Jan Muhammad that, in later life, he would beat people rather less than in his earlier years. (9).

Besides such insights into his personality, there are also many short passages here and there in the 'Teachings' which cast light on verses in Khwaja Farid's Diwan, and help us to see the very close inter-relationship between his talk and his poetry. To take only one example, the reference to the mispronunciation of 'sh' as 's' by the Prophet's muezzin, Bilal, in Lesson 18, immediately recalls the line 'Bilal's 's' was certainly 'sh' (*Diwan-e-Farid* 110,3). It is, however, in the matchless Lesson 19, where the Khwaja raises the storm in the one miracle directly witnessed by Rukn ud-Din, that we come closest to the magical creativity of his greatest hymns, which sing of the all-pervading presence of God. Supremely manifested in the spectacle of the rains coming to the parched desert. The book would, indeed, be worth having for this one Lesson alone.

Little needs to be said of the translation, which is intended only to bring this fascinating account to the attention of a modern readership in as comprehensible terms as possible. This aim has involved a considerable shortening of the author's pious formulas and honorific phrases, especially in the introductory biography quoted above and in the Prologue to the Lessons. Otherwise, only very occasional cuts have been made, the most notable being the omission of most of the quotations from law-books made in Rukn ud-Din's personal aside in Lesson 6.

English equivalents have been sought wherever possible for all Islamic words and technical terms of Sufism. Such expressions as 'spiritual director' do not, however, provide satisfactory equivalents for 'pir' or 'Shaikh', and these words have accordingly been retained, as have on occasion the honorific terms 'Hazrat' and 'Qibla'. Otherwise, though, it has been preferred to speak of a pir having a chosen 'successor' (*Sajjada-nishin*) appointed from among the 'deputies' (*Khalifa*), to whom he has granted a '*licence*' of spiritual of spiritual authority (*Ijazat*): similarly, ordinary 'disciples' (*Murid*) are said to take a 'vow of allegiance' (*bai'at*) to their pir, or to attend an 'anniversary festival' ('urs) at the tomb of the founder of their pir's spiritual 'line' (*Silsila*).

All quotations from the Holy Quran have been verified with the original and with the standard translations, and supplied with numerical references. All dates have been provided with their CE equivalents in brackets. In referring to these, it is important to remember that Rukn ud-Din reckons the day in the classical Muslim fashion as beginning at sunset, not at midnight as now. This explains the reference to Wednesday beginning at sunset in Lesson 13, or such apparent discrepancies as the same CE date being provided for two successive A.H. dates in the headings to Lessons 5 and 6.

THE POEMS

Khwaja Farid's stature as a Muslim of the firmest orthodoxy, a scholar with wide intellectual interests, a spiritual dignitary of real prestige, and a mystic of the rarest quality is undisputed. Add to these his romantic sensitivity to beauty and his magical ability to handle language, and you will have some idea of how rich and varied the poetry that issued from such a personality was bound to be.

In the poetry as in the personality, however, this variety is balanced by a harmonious sense of unity. We have suggested that this was only made possible by a favourable historical environment in which the unity world-view of classical Islamic civilization was still preserved from pressing external challenge. At the simplest level, this unity of Khwaja Farid's poetry emerges in his use of a single form, the traditional *kafi*, a rhymed poem of several verses with repeated refrain, perfectly designed for musical performance. There are 271 of these *kafis* recognized as constituting the most authentic body of Khwaja Farid's poetry, although he is also credited with a varying number of poems in different formal patterns. Our present selection of 50 *kafis* has been made from the standard edition of Aziz ur Rahman published with an extensive prose commentary in Bahawalpur in 1944. Thanks again to Khwaja Farid's relatively recent date, we are fortunate in possessing a reliable text of his poetry, whereas the poems of many of his great predecessors have had to be compiled from less trustworthy oral traditions.

The unity of the poetry emerges in another way also, for it is essentially timeless. Only rarely is it possible to date the poems by reference to external events. This is most obviously the case with the set of poems inspired by the author's performance of the pilgrimage in 1875-76, illustrated here by no.14; *On approaching Medina*. The unique *Ode to Sadiq Khan*, no.17, can also be assigned to 1879, when the ruler formally ascended the throne on attaining his majority.

Otherwise, at least until more detailed work is done on the chronology of Khwaja Farid's life, we have little idea of the order in which the poems were composed, or which were the most fruitful periods of his creativity. One might suppose, for instance, that the simplest poems are the earliest and the more complex ones were written towards the end of his life, but this is hardly a reliable method of procedure. It is in fact falsified anyway by such evidence as we do possess. The first printed version of the *kafis*, a very incomplete and unreliable edition printed in Benares in 1882, certainly contains a fair proportion of the more abstruse poems. Nos. 1, 9, 12, 20, 21, 31, 32, 34, and 38 of this book appear in the first edition, so these poems at least may be dated to the earlier part of Khwaja Farid's life.

A more profitable method of analysis is to examine the internal make-up of the poems themselves. Instead of being hampered by a shortage of information, we are here rather confronted by a super-abundant richness of evidence. Much has been written and will continue to be written about ways in which the poems can be analysed and classified, depending on the viewpoint of the critic. Here I want only to suggest a few broad categories which may be helpful in appreciating more fully the selected poems which are presented here.

In the first place, it must always be remembered that these are poems. Moreover, they are poems which are designed to be heard as songs if they are to have their full emotional effect. It is true that they are the work of a religious mind, profound both in its learning and its mystical awareness, but it would be a mistake to treat them as straightforward didactic messages. If one is chiefly interested in this aspect of Khwaja Farid's significance, the prosaic records compiled by his disciples will be found to provide far more direct access. Some of the poems, especially those in the earlier part of this book, do certainly contain direct teachings, but they are teachings emotionally apprehended and emotionally patterned, so that they need to be experienced through the emotions rather than the intellect. In the same way, the more obviously lyrical poems which occupy the later pages of this book should first be experienced directly as lyrics. Many passages are certainly capable of allegorical interpretation, for the appeal of these poems, like that of great poetry in any language, is based in part on the resonances of ambiguity which the richness of their expression sets up. The famous poem no.50 The *pilu-pickers*, has for instance been interpreted as an elaborate allegory in which the pilu-fruit symbolises the message of Islam and the various harvesters different classes of Muslims. Such exegesis can add to the reader's appreciation of the poem, but should not be allowed to limit it. After all, the commentary is secondary to poem, and while a single poem can inspire pages of critical analysis, the process is not reversible.

The second thing to remember is that these are poems of a special kind, given their formal structure as *kafis* and the literary tradition associated with this poetic form. The *kafi* is typically somewhat intermediate in status between the classic shorter forms of European poetry, with their emphasis on unity of mood, and the major vehicle of Muslim art-poetry, the ghazal, with its discrete series of couplets, which need bear little semantic relationship to one another. The *kafi* naturally approaches the ghazal more closely in most respects, but its greater simplicity and the use of the repeated refrain both tend to encourage an overall unity of mood. This is certainly true of Khwaja Farid's *kafis*, and I have sought to indicate where the centre of this unity lies by providing each English version with a title, in most cases derived from a particularly telling phrase in the poem. These titles are of course absent in the original.

Printed editions of the original follow the traditional pattern of alphabetical arrangement by the last letter of the rhyme. In order to provide a more direct path to immediate appreciation of the poetry in English, the poems have been grouped loosely by subject here, the traditional order being given in the Index of Siraiki first lines at the end of the book. The poems selected for inclusion have been grouped into three broad sections.

In the first part, called 'Poems of Faith and Instruction', will be found the most direct expressions of the ideas which inspired Khwaja Farid. The centre of this inspiration lies in his adherence to the Sufi doctrine of the unity of being, according to which nothing—if rightly regarded—is separate from God, who may be directly apprehended through one's own heart. This is certainly no easy process, as the suffering endured by those who attempt to follow this mystical path of love so clearly shows. But the alternative is to be lost in the most serious of sins, the separation from God and imprisonment in a false picture of self-identity, which stem from the dualism of self-esteem. The first few poems in the book express the poet's rejection of this way of thinking, and the final poems of the first part extol different human objects of the Khwaja's religious devotion.

The central section, 'Lyrics of Love and Distress', consists of poems in which what has been directly expressed in the first part now finds its emotional reflection in the experiences of the poet's heart. In keeping with the local tradition of the *kafi*, he now speaks through the persona of a young girl abandoned by her lover, who goes through varied emotional states of despair and resolve, dwelling on her past joys, bewailing her present unhappy state, and making plans to rejoin the one she loves.

The third section, named 'Songs of the Desert and the Rains', begins with poems describing the torments of the burning desert endured by Sassi, most famous of the local legendary heroines. Then the mood changes, and the joyful emotions evoked in the poet's heart by the spectacle of the newly blooming desert in the rainy season are described in a wonderfully fresh set of poems. This originality continues in the final poems, which are particularly associated with the romantic figure of Haram Mai Hotan.

A slightly more detailed description of the poems will be found in the short introductions to each part of the book. Of course, the division between the three parts is in no way absolute and themes and images criss-cross amongst themselves backwards and forwards throughout the poetry.

The inventory of these themes is a traditional one, drawn on by all Farid's predecessors, if less deeply than he was able to. I have given a broad picture of the nature of these elements in a short study of the earlier Siraiki poets Sachal Sarmast and Bedil Faqir, *Styles and themes in the Siraiki Mystical Poetry of Sind*, also published by Bazm-e-Saqafat. The repertoire essentially consists on the one hand of the teaching of Islamic mysticism and its classical literary expression in the formalised medium of the Persian Sufi ghazal, on the other of the conventions of local folk-poetry, in particular those associated with the girl forsaken by her lover, who may be further personified as one of the well-known heroines of the local romantic legends. Since these characters are alluded to by Khwaja Farid for the associative value of their emotional symbolism rather than as fully fledged characters in a lengthy narrative, their stories do not need to be once again retold at length here. The necessary details will be found in a summary form in the Index of Names which follows the poems.

When contrasted with the poetry of his predecessors, Khwaja Farid's originality is seen to lie only partly in the introduction of fresh material into the traditional repertoire. Sometimes, of course, he is original, as in the famous desert-poems, which directly reflect his own experience of the coming of the rains and burgeoning of fresh life in the sands. Often, however, what may seem original is but a fine development of what has gone before. The poems which vividly describe the terrors of the desert faced by the desperate Sassi nos. 37-39, for instance, derive largely from Lutf Ali's Siraiki narrative poem, the *Saifalnama* (itself based on an original in the *Arabian Nights*), of which Khwaja Farid is known to have been an admirer. Of course, he does surpass his model, but this illustration may serve to show where his real originality typically lies. It is in the encyclopaedic use which he made of all parts of the traditional repertoire, and the seemingly effortless fashion in which he was able to combine and juxtapose its elements into fresh patterns.

The result is the kind of all-embracing poetic language which can perhaps emerge only once in the history of any given literature. The rainbows certainly continue to glitter in the sky and the lines of camels to cross the dunes in the pages of his successors, who find themselves his helpless imitators. But for all their reiteration of the sweetness of the sounds of cattle-bells or drizzling rain, that rich and allusive magic which is the hallmark of Khwaja Farid's style can no longer quite exert the same spell.

Even greater, of course, are the difficulties involved in the attempt to convey something of Khwaja Farid's poetic art in such a radically different medium as English. These difficulties have indeed been sufficient to discourage me from the task for some twelve years, since I first encountered his poetry. The basic problem is that English is so different from Siraiki, both in the formal structures and in its literary traditions, so that there is little possibility of readily producing close equivalents of the original, as there usually is in such more nearly related languages as Urdu.

Unless the translator is himself a born poet, the business of translation will have to be begun by making more or less arbitrary decisions and seeking more or less mechanical solutions. It will have to be recognized at the outset that it will not be possible to reproduce some features of the original at all in the translated version. Khwaja Farid, for instance, while basically composing in his native Siraiki, also drew freely on forms from the language of central Punjab. He was clearly fascinated by languages, and introduces all sorts of forms and phrases from other tongues to add to the richness and variety of his poetry. These may be sacred quotations from the Arabic, as in no.6, or a deliberate mixture of two different languages, as in no.31, which is a macaronic, having alternate verses in Persian and Siraiki. Other poems are written in more or less pure forms of other languages: thus no.5 is basically in Urdu, no.13 in Sindhi, and no.41 in Brajbhasha. There is no way in which linguistic variety on this scale can be happily reproduced in translation, but its abandonment means that part of the quality of the original has already been sacrificed.

Conscious and often difficult decisions do have to be made as to whether other, more basic features will be reproduced or not. The most obvious of these is the regular prosodic framework of the *kafi*, its strict patterns of metre and rhyme. It is obviously easier to disregard these, and this is the solution adopted by Professor Gilani Kameran and Aslam Ansarie in the only substantial translation of Khwaja Farid's poetry into English so far to have been published, by Bazm-e-Saqafat in 1969. Their version is in a kind of free verse, which is sometimes very effective, but too often introduces a loose discursiveness which is at odds with the tightly organized expression of the original.

Since this expression is often closely determined by the formal patterns of the *kafi*, it seemed worth making the attempt to reproduce these fairly closely here. The easiest of these patterns to convert into English is the meter. The Siraiki *kafi* is written in a regular accentual meter very much more similar to the typical patterns of English poetry than to the meters of Urdu poetry, depending on syllable length and derived, through Persian, ultimately from Arabic. In the commonest and most basic meter a line with four accented syllables is followed by one with three. This goes very well into English, with a shift of the accent from the first to the second syllable. Take for instance the well-known verse from poem no.47:

/ *ratin* / *karin shi-* / *kar di-* / *lin de*
/ *dinhan va-* / *lorin* / *mattian*

The rhythm of the English is very similar:

By / night they / hunt for / lovers' / hearts:
They / churn their / pots by / day.

Nearly all the *kafis* are written in variants of this common meter, although with his usual inventiveness Khwaja Farid created many fresh patterns within the basic prosodic framework of lines of four and three beats. The same sort of English meter also suits the few poems composed in simple meters of the Urdu type, like the hazaj of no.31. Khwaja Farid occasionally used a much longer metrical line, and I have tried to give some idea of this in no.42.

The great advantage of a fairly strict reproduction of the original meter is that it discourages the translator's chief temptation, which is to pad out the original and lengthen it with his own explanations. The conciseness of Khwaja Farid's expression is an important part of its appeal, and is greatly weakened by over-diffuse translation. The demands of English grammar have often compelled me to add an extra syllable to the line, but the number of lines is always the same as in the original. I have sometimes deliberately altered the meter for the sake of variety, as in my versions of no.23 and 46, which are in anapaests, with two unaccented syllables between each beat. Extra unaccented syllables have similarly sometimes between slipped into one line of each verse, as in nos. 2 and 22. With minor adjustments of this type, there are relatively few *kafis* which it is not possible to provide with reasonable English metrical versions.

The next problem is a more serious one—what should be done about the rhyme? I had previously tried my hand at producing unrhymed English verse translations of Siraiki *kafis*, as in the few versions of Sachal Sarmast included in my introduction to the Bazm-e-Saqafat selection of his poetry, and was strongly tempted to follow a similar pattern here. The word '*kafi*' is often said to be derived from the Arabic qawafi, meaning 'rhymes', and (whatever the truth of the matter) it is certainly true that the *kafi* fairly bristles with rhymes, which come much more easily in Siraiki than they do in English. The last line of each verse always has the same rhyme as the refrain, and in the more complex verse-patterns favoured or invented by Khwaja Farid, the other lines of each verse usually rhyme with each other as well.

Since rhyme has such an important place in the formal scheme of the *kafi*, it seemed on reflection hardly possible to claim that the quality of the original was really being faithfully reproduced in unrhymed versions. Khwaja Farid was certainly too good a poet usually to allow his expression to be dictated by the rhyme, but on the other hand the rhyme often gives a point and finality to the expression which just seems flat and meaningless in rhymed English.

The attempt has accordingly been made to produce English translations whose rhyme-schemes will at least approximate to the original, especially in the most important feature of the main rhyme at the end of the refrain and each verse, which is the single most powerfully unifying formal feature of the *kafi*. The rule to reproduce this main rhyme in all cases has of course meant that it has not always been possible to include poems here which certainly deserve translation, but which defy efforts to find a satisfactory rhyme. This particularly applies to the longer *kafis*, where the abundance of rhyming words in Siraiki, particularly when amplified by Khwaja Farid's fondness for freely adopting words from other languages, simply cannot be matched by English. There is, therefore, a bias towards the shorter poems here, the one with the greatest number of verses being no.11. Considerations of rhyme have not, however, been allowed seriously to affect the overall aim of giving a representative selection of the different themes on which Khwaja Farid's *kafis* are composed.

There is also a reasonable selection of *kafis* in different formal patterns. In the simplest type, naturally well represented, the lines simply rhyme .a, .a, .a. Then there are those of three-line verses, typically rhyming bba, cca, dda, as in no. 29, or .ba, .ba, .ba, as in no. 19, both reproduced in English. In *kafis* with verses of four lines each, various rhyming patterns are encountered. The easiest to reproduce in English are those where there is no regular internal rhyme, like no. 5, where the verses simply rhyme . . .a, . . .a, . . .a. The commonest type, however, illustrated by no. 8, has the rhyme bbba, ccca, ddda, which is kept in English. In a third variation, the verses rhyme ccba, ddba, eeba, which is reproduced in English in no. 12. Elsewhere, however, I have left the third line unrhymed, as in no. 50, whose fame demanded its inclusion, but where it proved impossible to keep both the sense and the rhyme of the original. Finally, there is one example of a *kafi* in six line verses, no. 24, regularly rhyming .b.b.a, .c.c.a, .d.d.a. In all types of *kafi* the refrain often varies slightly both in the meter and in internal rhyme from the main pattern, and I have taken full advantage of this licence in the translations. To distinguish it from the rest of the poem, the refrain is printed in different type.

The rhymes in the original are usually feminine, containing two syllables, the second of which is as often as not a grammatical ending. Masculine rhymes of one syllable are less frequent. Triple rhymes are also occasionally used. In English, with its abundance of vowel-sounds and greatly reduced grammatical structure, it is simply impossible to find an adequate number of feminine rhymes. All the main rhymes are accordingly of one syllable only, although I have sometimes used feminine rhymes within the verses, as in nos. 9 and 32. The use of masculine rhymes in place of feminine fits naturally with the shifting of the rhythmic accent described earlier.

All English translators who use rhyme find that they need all the help they can get, and I have not hesitated to employ all the usual devices. These include the alteration of the order of lines within a verse, poetic inversions of word order, and the occasional use of eye-rhymes. Assonance rather than true rhyme has sometimes been used, often helped by the presence at the end of the line of the typical repeated term of address, so frequently found in the *kafi*, as in nos. 37 and 39. It should perhaps be said that the rhymes are based on my own version of standard British English, in which a final –r, for instance, is not pronounced, but simply colours the quality of the preceding vowel.

The only other formal convention of the *kafi* which calls for remark is the regular inclusion of the poet's name in the final verse. This typical feature of most types of Islamic and Indian poetry is not one which always reproduces very happily in English, and I have been quite arbitrary in my treatment of it here. It is sometimes included, where it seemed to fit naturally, but is just as frequently omitted.

Other features of Farid's poetry cannot be dealt with by general rules, but must be solved in individual ways, depending upon the particular context. Alliteration and playing on words are, for example, important parts of his poetic technique. These can sometimes be reproduced where they occur in the original, but more often than not have to be passed over. Here, though, especially so far as alliteration is concerned, it is often possible to give the right overall impression of his style by putting it in where it fits the English more naturally.

Finally, there are two general areas of great difficulty through which the translator of Khwaja Farid must make his way as best he can. These both concern his poetic vocabulary. The first lines in the semantic area of what may be called 'the language of love', and is a problem very generally faced in the translation of Oriental poetry into a Western language like English. The rich conventions of the

Persian ghazal provide an immense ready-made collection of words associated with love, which convey the lover's pain and distress and the beloved's beauty and cruelty in time-honoured images with many interlocking impressionistic associations between them. So close are these associations that the language is almost a code, which it is extraordinarily difficult to break and convert into English. Khwaja Farid's language, in which Siraiki synonyms are freely used alongside the Persian and Arabic words of the ghazal, is still more difficult to reproduce, and I am very conscious of the shortcomings of my attempts at finding satisfactory English equivalents.

The second area of difficulty is in a sense the reverse of the first. This concerns Khwaja Farid's use of specific local terminology, rather than his generalized emotional vocabulary. The most obvious instance of this is in his very extensive use of terms associated with the natural phenomena of the desert, and with the life of the nomad tribesmen. This of course presents problems even to translators working in such a closely related language as Urdu. The only possible solutions are to keep the original words and provide footnotes on their meaning, or else to find loose English equivalents. I have generally preferred the latter way out, even though this all too often means that the sharply detailed imagery of the original poems in the third part of this book is blurred and generalised. There are, accordingly, very few footnotes to translations.

As I have already said, these poems are after all songs, and if my translations convey something of this quality to the reader, they will have succeeded in their aim.

The Teachings

of Khwaja Ghulam Farid

Author's Prologue

In the name of God, the Compassionate, the Merciful

I, the humble Rukn ud-Din, son of Muhammad, son of Muhammad Alam, son of Muhammad Murad, known as Pirhar, Sonaki by my place of origin, Hanafi by adherence, and Chishti by spiritual allegiance, crave the Pardon of God for myself and my ancestors, and His blessing on my descendants.

Be it known that these few pages comprise a fresh and new collection, to be read by one and all with great benefit and enjoyment, of the noble utterances of the greatest and holiest saint of our age, Khwaja Ghulam Farid.

Be it also known that by reason of the distance of my abode and the pressures of my affairs, I have been unable to keep constant attendance upon the holy Khwaja. But on those occasions when I have been granted the honour of being admitted to his presence, I have memorised all that I heard and witnessed, and recorded this in these pages. The book has been called '*The Teachings of Farid*', or 'The Lessons of the Meetings'; for each Lesson will be found to cast the most wonderful light on different aspects of faith and mystical religion.

Lesson 1: Great Sufi Texts
Tuesday, 19th Rajab, A.H. 1302 (4.5.1885)

I was granted the supreme blessing of humble attendance upon the holy Khwaja in the evening.

I was studying the *Sitta Maratib* together with Makhdum Ghulam Shah of Uch, the brother of Hazrat Makhdum Wilayat Shah. After the lesson, the soul was discussed, and the Khwaja said, 'After its separation from this dark and coarse physical body, the soul is joined to the light and delicate spiritual body, where it changes and develops.'

Then he said, 'The *Tuhfa-e-Mursala* is a book to be revered for many reasons. Not only is it the work of Shaikh Abu Sai'd Makhzumi, the pir of the great saint Shaikh Abdul Qadir Gilani, but it was according to its author—actually written for his spiritual son, Shaikh Abdul Qadir.' He then explained why the book was called the *Tuhfa-e-Mursala*, or "The Gift sent to the Prophet", saying that its author had composed it as an offering to the spirit of the Holy Prophet.

'But our mullahs,' he continued, 'say that it is a work of unbelief to write books about the mysteries of pure monism and the unity of being. That saintly author dedicates what he has written to the Holy Prophet, and they—God save the mark!—say that this is against Islam.' This remark prompted me to say, with hands humbly folded, 'How unfortunate they are to be unable to distinguish the very foundations of faith from unbelief! Their idle words in fact go against obedience to God and the Law of the Holy Prophet. They are shown up as being foolish and ridiculous!'

'Yes,' said the Khwaja, 'as someone who recognized the glory of the noble company of mystics said:

> What shall I say in praise of that great saint?
> He is no Prophet, yet he has a Book!'

The Khwaja also briefly explained the meaning of these verses by saying, 'It would be improper to call that Prince of saints, Maulana Jalal-ud-Din Rumi, a prophet, for he appeared after the glorious manifestation of the Seal of the Prophets. But his book, the holy Masnawi, is such a rich store of mystical truths that it is, one might say, on a level with revealed scriptures as the Torah, Gospels and Psalms. Since this level was not attained by the books of other saints, the rank of Maulana Rumi is unique and unparalleled.'

LESSON 2: STORIES OF MAULAVI MUHAMMAD HAMID AND KHWAJA KHUDA BAKHSH
MONDAY, 8TH SAFAR, A.H. 1311 (21.8.1893)

I was granted the supreme blessing of humble attendance upon the holy Khwaja in the middle of the morning.

After making general inquiries about my well-being, such as one asks of anyone who has come from far away, and as was a custom most carefully observed by the Khwaja, he asked me, 'How are you getting on, and how is it that you have come?' 'Lord,' I replied, 'Maulavi Abdur Rahman, the son of Maulavi Nur-ud-Din of Fatehpur, who was the teacher of your humble servant, has died. His brother and successor, Maulavi Abdus Sattar, has come to attend upon you, that you may grant him your attention and bestow upon him your spiritual direction, and that he may take his place as a full member of your noble company.'

On hearing my news, an expression of grief overshadowed the glorious countenance of the Khwaja, and he said how deeply sorry he was. Then he turned to Maulavi Abdus Sattar, who was sitting next to me, and inquired of him, 'Up to what text have you studied Arabic, and under which teacher?' 'I have studied up to the *Sharh-e-Mullah*,' he replied, 'under the late Maulavi Ali Muhammad, who is now deceased, God rest his soul!' The Khwaja again expressed his regret, and said, 'Maulavi Ali Muhammad was a good man.'

Thereupon one of those present in the company said, 'Maulavi Muhammad Hamid of Fatehpur was indeed a great saint. This is shown by the story which I have heard of how he once was in Medina, when someone recognising his quality, let him into the holy tomb of the Prophet in order to bring out a dead pigeon that was lying inside. 'This is not one of the better-known stories about him,' said the Khwaja, 'and I have never heard it told of him. On the other hand, the story of how the turban was given to him at the behest of the Holy Prophet is, of course, very well-known and popular—am I not right?' he asked me. 'Indeed, it is just as you say,' I replied. 'And what about the story of his being given the turban by the Holy Prophet?' he asked. 'Oh, there's no doubting that one,' I said, and related the story as I had heard it. The Khwaja then commented, 'It may be that the Prophet had declared in his will who the turban was to be given to, just as several saints have received his blessed combs.'

He then gave the authentic version of the story of the removal of the dead pigeon from the holy tomb. 'There was a young boy in Medina who was instructed to get the pigeon out. He was told that he would attain the highest wisdom by breaking upon the sacred tomb. Well, the boy did come out with the pigeon in his hand, but he had fallen into a trance and was unable to speak. On the third day he died in this same silent condition.'

The Khwaja then asked whether Maulavi Muhammad Hamid had been licensed by Hafiz Muhammad Jamal of Multan or by Khwaja Khuda Bakhsh of Khairpur. 'He was granted his licence of spiritual authority by Hafiz Jamal,' I answered, 'but, after the latter's death, he derived much spiritual benefit from his association with Khwaja Khuda Bakhsh.'

The Khwaja then went on, 'Khwaja Khuda Bakhsh of Khairpur was the appointed successor of Hafiz Jamal, but he used to show the greatest respect to his elder contemporary, Qazi Muhammad Isa of Khanpur, whom Hafiz Jamal had licensed as a deputy. Khwaja Khuda Bakhsh once asked him, "Shall I license you myself?" But the Qazi frowned, and said that it was hardly suitable for him to be licensed by a fellow-disciple of his pir. So the Khwaja went off, upset and distressed; but as he was on his way, the Qazi caught up with him, greeted him, and said, "Let me license you instead!" "Oh, how gracious and kind of you! Said the Khwaja, "I am fortunate indeed!" And so he asked his fellow-disciple to grant him his licence of authority and approval, saying, "This licence is exactly the same as that of my pir." Then he was pronounced licensed by the Qazi. From that day on he would say that anyone going to Khanpur had no need of Khairpur, while anyone coming to Khairpur had no need of Khanpur.'

Then he said, 'All the deputies of Hazrat Hafiz Jamal, although they had received their licence from the saint himself, always looked to Khwaja Khuda Bakhsh for their authority.'

LESSON 3: LEADING DEPUTIES OF LOCAL SAINTS
THURSDAY, 11TH SAFAR, A.H. 1311. (24.8.93)

I was granted the supreme blessing of humble attendance upon the holy Khwaja in the afternoon.

The deputies of Khwaja Muhammad Sulaiman of Taunsa were being discussed. The Khwaja said, 'It was Maulavi Muhammad Baran who surpassed all the other deputies of Khwaja Muhammad Sulaiman in both outward learning and inner knowledge. Three deputies were outstanding among those of three different saints,' he continued. These three were Maulavi Muhammad Baran, the greatest deputy of Khwaja Muhammad Baran; Khwaja Khuda Bakhsh of Khairpur, the chosen successor of Hafiz Muhammad Jamal of Multan; and Sultan Mahmud of Khanbela, the outstanding deputy of our own great Shaikh, Khwaja Muhammad Aqil.'

LESSON 4: PRIVATE INSTRUCTION OF RUKN UD DIN—
HIS BOOK APPROVED BY THE KHWAJA
TUESDAY, 11TH JUMADA I, A.H. 1311 (21.11.93)

I was granted the supreme blessing of humble attendance upon the holy Khwaja at noon.

Addressing all those who were present, the Khwaja said, 'Get up and go outside, for I have business with Rukn ud-Din.' When everyone had left, he most kindly summoned his humble creature to come over to him from the corner where he had been sitting. As soon as he beckoned me, I quickly rose and sat down before the Khwaja. He asked how I was, and told me to tell him everything. In my childish delight at having the blessed opportunity of this private audience, I poured out a detailed account of everything, good and bad, fair and foul, which had happened to me. Then, directing his blessed countenance towards the Holy Kaaba, and sitting in a kneeling position as at prayer, he bade me sit beside him in the same fashion. When I had done this, he began by instructing me afresh in some private devotional exercises, and then bestowed upon me all the hidden teachings of the mysteries which it has been my humble fortune to be given. These must not be divulged.

'Then befell what befell with one glimpse of his face.'

(If you want further details, you should consult the separate treatise called *Masalik-e-Faridi*).

He then asked if I would be able to get hold of the *Kimiya-e-Saadat* and the *Misbah-ul-Hidayat*. 'Certainly,' I replied, 'I have them at home.' 'Come back in two weeks,' he said. 'And bring both books with you, so that I can mark some passages in them for you to profit by in your reading. I will also get you to read another book from my own collection on Sufism and the Unity of being, which forms an essential part of the study of that noble discipline.'

Then I humbly said, 'Lord, my whole life has been wasted in idle pursuits, and spent in sins and evil deeds. It has been utterly devoid of pious practices like fasting, prayer, pilgrimage and alms-giving, and other good and noble things. Now that I have found refuge with my glorious pir, and gained a place in the shadow of his grace and favour, I desire to collect in a book all that I can remember of his holy words, glorious utterances, and noble qualities. I would regard such a collection as the instrument of my salvation, for I cannot conceive of any better harvest from this world which could serve as my provision on my journey to the next world.'

'First show me the pages you have written,' he replied, 'then I will tell you what I think of them.' Having thus been favoured with his permission, I departed for my home. Glory and praise be to God for the private audience so filled with blessing and grace which I had received!

On the appointed day, the 25th of the same month, I was privileged to come again before the Khwaja, who asked me if I had brought with me the books he had mentioned. I replied that I had, and humbly gave him them. At the same time I presented my noble teacher with the pages that I had written, comprising the first three Lessons.

So much for my description of what has already come to pass. That which later emerges from the unseen world will continue to be recorded in this memoir, if God so will!

LESSON 5: THE ISLAM OF THE SWEEPERS—THE FORGIVENESS OF THE SAINTS—UN-ISLAMIC CUSTOM—A MIRACLE OF BABA FARID—STORIES OF IMAM MUHAMMAD GHAZALI—ON SNUFF TAKING
WEDNESDAY, 26TH JUMADA I, A.H. 1311 (6.12.93)

I was granted the supreme blessing of humble attendance upon the holy Khwaja in the afternoon.

The Islamic faith of sweepers and other low castes was discussed. The Khwaja said, 'They are Muslims. All they have to do is to recognise the things permitted by God as lawful, those prohibited by Him as unlawful. It is true that they consume what is forbidden, but they do not try to make out that the unlawful is permitted, since they know full well what is prohibited and what is lawful. This confirms their sin, but not their unbelief. In the same way, habitual drunkards, adulterers, and so on, are sinners, but not unbelievers. The point can be summed up by saying that the perpetration of serious sins does not exclude one from the faith, unless one seeks to minimise them or to declare them lawful. It follows that sweepers are Muslims, although they are sinners because of their consumption of forbidden substances. This is particularly true of our sweepers, who do abstain from consuming forbidden food and other prohibited things, and who follow no occupation other that sweeping. No suspicion or doubt can be applied to their Islam, for sweeping is not a necessary condition of unbelief.'

The subject then changed to the glorious virtues of the holy company of saints. The Khwaja said, 'Once there was a servant of the great Khwaja Nizam-ud-Din Badauni, who had spent his entire life mocking and grumbling against the saint. Although he would hear his evil talk, the holy Khwaja would not say anything in regard to that miserable wretch. Then the fellow died. When news of his death was brought to the saint, he took his staff in his hand and arose that very instant to go to the scoffer's grave, where he offered a double prayer of super-erogation. After completing this, he prostrated himself, and privately besought the Granter of all prayers, saying, "O Lord of the two worlds, no matter what this man has said about me, do not charge him with sin on this account. I have re-signed my claims against him. Do you also, in your All-embracing Mercy, pardon him. And I beseech You, by this white beard which I am rubbing in the dust in earnest supplication, to forego any claims which you may have against him."'

Then he went on to speak of the unrivalled magnificence of the state kept by Hazrat Mahbub-e-Ilahi, the scale of whose expense could be judged by the story that a train of 40 camels, or even more, used to be loaded with the onion skins that had been peeled in a single day for his kitchens, on their way to be thrown outside the town.

'One day,' he went on, 'a beggar appeared in the holy assembly of the Shaikh, and addressed him, saying, "Bestow an abundance of gold upon me, for I am poor and needy, and you are rich!" Now this speech was accompanied by all manner of ill-mannered, unseemly and wounding words. The Shaikh, however, said nothing. In fact, he gazed upon him kindly with a happy expression on his face. The others present in the assembly were, of course, entirely filled with feelings of humility and self-abasement, prepared, like moths round a candle, to sacrifice their lives for the Shaikh. When they saw the saint thus cheerful and careless, not bothering to reprove the beggar who said such idle and foolish things, they were upset and visibly distressed. Anyway, the Shaikh asked, "What do you want, my son?" "Twenty *mohurs* of gold," he said. Then the holy Khwaja bestowed forty mohurs of gold upon him, before dismissing him. The others said, "Lord he reviled and insulted you, yet your Eminence actually granted him an increase of twenty mohurs over and above that he had demanded. What mystery lies behind this surprising action?" There are two reasons he replied. "In the first place, I am a man just like you, one of the humble creatures of Almighty God, possessing no superior gifts or quality. What knowledge I have is surpassed by your greater learning and accomplishments. Yet, in spite of this, you all fall at my feet, and praise and magnify me. So, in terms of thanks for this exalted position of mine, the twenty extra mohurs which I gave him count for nothing at all. The second reason is that the fellow made me aware of the faults in my soul, so that was most worthy and deserving of the gift of abundant gold, and what I gave him was but little in comparison with his deserts.

The next subject to be discussed was the condemnation of customs prevalent in all parts of society, which are against the Law. The holy Khwaja said, 'Disgraceful customs contrary to the Law have become widespread throughout the land that it has become exceedingly difficult to root them out—indeed the matter has gone beyond the bounds of possibility. Take, for example, the dress of the women of our country. The sleeves of their tunics come down only to the upper arm, leaving the rest bare. Very few veil their faces and bodies. Most of them let their veils hang behind their heads, exposing their face, both sides of their head, the arms and chest, and sit and parade shamelessly like this through the market and bazaars. Sometimes they proudly appear with their veils thrown over their shoulders before men who are not members of their family. A great many blameworthy and disgraceful customs are also current at weddings, as when men and women form a circle together and dance and jump about, clapping their hands, while the drum beats in the middle of the circle, not to speak of all the other forbidden and pernicious things that go on. All these disgusting habits and practices are Hindu customs, works of the infidels which are current also among Muslims, who take delight and enjoyment in them. If they are forbidden to continue, they reply, "Enough for us is what we found our fathers doing." (Quran, 5:104).

'Khwaja Muhammad Aqil,' he continued, 'that stern upholder of the Sunna, once went to Mahar Sharif to visit his great pir, Hazrat Qibla-e-Alam. When he reached that holy place, he found the Shaikh whose piety was without rival in that age, attending someone's wedding-feast, where every disgraceful custom imaginable was being observed in defiance of the Law. The saintly Khwaja then humbly asked his holy pir, "Lord, since you are the greatest Shaikh in the world, why do you not order the people to cease to observe these reprehensible practices, and make them come to obey Almighty God and the Holy Prophet?" "These foolish customs," explained the saint, "have taken such a powerful hold on ordinary people's hearts that, even if I were to succeed in making them give up these wanton and forbidden amusements, then, when by God's will some injury befell their goods or their children, they would say, 'This harm which has befallen our property and families is certainly due to our having abandoned those customs.'"

Such a heretical statement would mean that they were unbelievers, guilty of questioning the uniqueness of God, and so, instead of carrying on with these customs, whose practice is indeed a sin, they would stand convicted of polytheism, which is the worst sort of unbelief—may God save us from it! This is why I refrain from forbidding the people these actions, and have permitted them to continue.'''

At this point I asked with due humility, 'Lord, will those who perform customs unsanctioned by the Law be very severely chastised and punished, or not?' 'They will face the most evil reckoning,' he said. Then I asked, 'Is that which is ratified by religion and embraced by the bounds of the Law good and excellent, and does it lead one to the goal of one's desire?' 'Yes,' he answered 'that is the straight path. So anyone who steps aside from this way of salvation falls into the jungle of heresy and error.'

Then he said, 'There are indeed many works of the Devil, which are apparently good and pious while actually being evil and foul, so that anyone who performs them becomes a follower of Satan. For it is the habit of that eternally accursed evil being to conjure up wonderful temptations before the ignorant, and cast them into error and destruction. There is an old story which tells how the great Khwaja Farid-ud-Din of Ajodhya when a young man, was once travelling in the land of Marwar. In the course of his journeying, he chanced to pass by a great temple— that is, an idol-house of the infidels, where the idolaters used to worship—where he saw a man cut off his tongue and place it as an offering before an idol, while making endless supplications to it. Then he licked the walls, and his tongue became perfectly whole, so that one would not think it had ever been severed. Next he went to another idol and cut his tongue in the same fashion, placed it as an offering before the idol, and had no sooner licked the walls than his tongue was perfectly restored. Each time that evil trickster enacted this amazing performance, he was eagerly followed by a wondering crowd of ignorant and simple people. But the holy saint realized through the light of his secret inner knowledge that this was Satan the accursed, who was drawing the people to himself and leading them astray, by beguiling them with this fraudulent piece of jugglery. So he went up to him, and murmured in his ear, "You are Satan the deceitful. Be on your way, and go where you will, but do not mislead and destroy the creatures of God!" And, in sorrow and shame, he was forced to confess and acknowledge his devilishness.'

Books of mysticism were then talked about, and somebody said 'Lord, would you say something about the *Ihya-ul-Ulum*, that excellent book which deals so sublimely with the mysteries, so that everyone may have the happiness of studying it?'

'Yes,' said the holy Khwaja, 'there is an obligation—indeed, a sacred duty to study three books, dear to all mystical seekers, which represent the quintessence of the way. It has been the custom of our great Shaikh to tell all those who seek to find God to study these three books. One the *Misbah-ul-Hidayat*, the translation of the *Awarif-ul-Maarif*, the second is the *Ihya-ul-Ulum*, and the third is its abridged version, the *Kimiya-e-Saadat*, which is a recipe of wondrous healing for anyone who possesses the least smattering of real knowledge.'

'The author of the last two,' he went on, 'was the great Imam Muhammad Ghazali, the "Proof of Islam". There is a well-known story, which has been passed down through the centuries, about him and the Prophet Moses^AS. Moses^AS once petitioned the court of Almighty God that he might meet and talk with one of the learned men of the community of the Prophet Muhammad^S.A.W. A great debate and disputation then took place in the spiritual world. Moses^AS asked him his name, and he answered, "Muhammad, the son of Muhammad, Ghazali.' "You talk too much," said Moses^AS. "No, I don't," he said, "for you are a man, just like me, and it is obvious that a man does not possess knowledge of what is hidden. Just as you did not know my name, so you were ignorant of my father's name, and of the name of the place I come from. If I had told you only my own name, you still would have wanted to ask me further what my father's name was, and where I came from. So my answer was intended to cover everything I considered to be implied by your question. Actually, if you really want to know, you are the one who talks too much, inasmuch as when God asked you, 'What is that, Moses, thou hast in thy right hand?', you said, 'Why, it is my staff. I lean upon it, and walk with it. I beat down leaves to feed my sheep; other uses also I find in it?' (Quran, 20: 17–18). When Almighty God, who knows what is invisible as well as what is visible, asked you what you had in your hand, it would have been sufficient to reply, 'It is my staff.' The rest of your reply was both wordy and impolite, being quite uncalled-for by the question." Now when he heard this, Moses^AS was enraged, in spite of his awesome self-control, and slapped the Imam on the cheek. And it is said that the Imam was born with one side of his face red as a result of the blow.'

'His brother, Shaikh Ahmad Ghazali,' the Khwaja continued, 'had a much higher rank as a mystic than the "Proof of Islam". He was the founder of many Sufi orders. The Kubrawi, Suhrawardi, Nurbakhshi and Madyani orders all stem from him, whereas no order stems from the Proof of Islam; for he obtained the robe of sainthood for himself, and bore it off with him, without bestowing it on anybody else. There is a story which tells how one day someone asked Shaikh Ahmad where his brother, Imam Muhammad, was, and what he was doing. "He is drowning in blood," he said. The questioner went to look for him, and found him in the mosque. Astonished by what Shaikh Ahmad had said, he repeated his conversation to the great Imam, who said, "My brother spoke the truth, for I was here reflecting on a problem of the Law concerned with a woman who bleeds after her period is over." This action of his brother the Imam, explained the Khwaja, 'who used to follow his own judgment in the branches of the Law, was unpleasing to Shaikh Ahmad. That is why he said, "He is drowning in blood." For the Proof of Islam was one of the pious while Shaikh Ahmad was one of the saints, and what the pious think good the saints may think evil.'

Then he said of course, Imam Muhammad Ghazali was, in his own right, one of the greatest Shaikhs of his time, and one of the most famous scholars of the Muslim community. This is why he was awarded the title of the "Proof of Islam".

One of those present in the company then asked which saint Imam Muhammad was spiritually linked to, and the Khwaja replied, 'The pir of the proof of Islam was Shaikh Abu Ali Farmadi, and the pir of Shaikh Ahmad Ghazali was Shaikh Abu Bakr Nassaj. Both these Shaikhs were disciples of Hazrat Abul Qasim Gorgani. But just think how Imam Muhammad Ghazali, who died at the age of 64, managed in so short a time to perfect his mastery over all branches of learning! Besides spending a good deal of time in teaching, in developing fresh positions in the Law, and in devoting himself to mortification and contemplation, he also composed many standard works of great value on every subject, such as his commentary, the *Yqut-ul-Tawil*, written in 40 volumes, the *Jawahir-ul-Quran*, the *Ihya-ul-Ulum*, the *Kimiya-e-Saadat*, and the Mishkat-ul-Anwar, as well as many others. To write so many books must be accounted a miracle, for how else could a human being write so much? In a similar fashion, the works of the Great Shaikh, Hazrat Muhyud Din Ibn-ul-Arabi, are 500 in number according to one account or, in the most extreme version, amount to 3,005. This extraordinary fecundity must be reckoned a manifest miracle with no natural explanation.'

'In the introduction to his *Fusus-ul-Hikam*,' he remarked, 'the Great Shaikh announces that everything he had composed or compiled, he heard directly from the Holy Prophet,[S.A.W] and then reduced this to writing.' I then asked, 'Lord, is it true or not that the saints act by divine command in writing their books?' The Khwaja replied, 'The words "What he speaks of the Divine Being all derives from divine inspiration", originally applied to the Holy Prophet,[S.A.W.] are also a command which governs the great saints and Sufis, and one's words and deeds issue from the command of Almighty God.'

Later, the lawfulness or otherwise of taking snuff was talked about, and the Khwaja said that it was not a good thing. I said 'It is said in the *Darr-ul-Mukhtar* of Shaikh Najm-ud-Din Kubra that tobacco is forbidden because it acts as a tranquilizer, and all substances which intoxicate or tranquilize are forbidden.' Then the Khwaja said, 'The taking of snuff is blameworthy, but not forbidden. Although I myself do take snuff, I am not addicted to it. If I give it up, it causes me no distress. When I set out on the pilgrimage to the Hejaz, I gave up snuff, and from that time until my return I did not resume the habit. Whenever I entered the Holy Sanctuary, I would say to my companions who were powerfully addicted to the use of snuff, "This is the holy spot where the angels descended, and where the divine mysteries were made manifest. It contains the memorials of the Best of Men and Prophets, and its holy inner court is free from the dust of polytheism, heresy, and unbelief. One is, therefore, obliged to refrain from taking snuff from the moment of entering the holy precinct until one comes out." And they, carrying out my instructions, did so refrain from taking snuff.'

LESSON 6: PRAYING ON WOOL—PRAYER WRITTEN FOR DISCIPLES
THURSDAY, 27TH JUMADA I, A.H. 1311 (6.12.03)

I was granted the supreme blessing of humble attendance upon the holy Khwaja in the evening.

The Khwaja asked a maulavi who was present for his opinion of the lawfulness of performing the prayer on a woollen cloth. He answered, 'In the *Sharh-e-Wiqaya* it is said that "Worship on wool is disapproved". When the Khwaja asked me for my opinion, I replied that I was well aware of what the legal position was. Then he said, 'It is permitted to offer prayers upon a woollen cloth and to perform one's prostrations on it. No disapproval attaches to this.' Turning towards me, he asked, 'Do you remember how woollen carpets were laid out in the Holy Sanctuary of the Prophet,[S.A.W.] notwithstanding the presence of great legal scholars and experts from every land and region, and how they used to offer prayer on them? If they had considered this practice to be disapproved of, they would certainly have refrained from it.

In the opinion of the Shias,' he went on, 'it is not permissible to prostrate oneself on anything other than the ground. I have myself seen Shias in the Holy Sanctuary who, if they happened to be standing on a carpet, would move off it to lay their heads in prostration on the ground. That is to say that at the moment of prostration they would keep their feet and knees on the carpet, while stretching out their necks to prostrate their foreheads on the patches of ground left between the carpets on account of the pillars.'

Here I would offer a reproof—may God confirm my sincerity and faith—the phrase 'Worship on wool is disapproved' does not actually occur in the *Sharh-e-Wiqaya*, nor in fact in any other standard authority, such as the *Kanz-ul-Daqaiq* (including several commentaries upon it), the *Durr-ul-Mukhtar,* the *Jami-ur-Rauza,* or the *Hidaya*. So it is impossible to tell what the maulavi can have been thinking of when he dared to give a legal opinion based on a phrase made up by himself in the presence of the greaest authority on the Law of his time. I can supply quotations from several legal works to show that praying upon woollen carpets or cloth is lawful, and not disapproved of. To take just one example, it is written in the *Fatwas of Qazi Khan* that 'There is no harm in offering prayer on carpets, rugs, or floor-coverings of felt, although it is best to offer prayer upon the earth, and upon what the earth brings forth.' This and other passages make it clear that the great blessing of prayer does not become abhorrent by being offered on wool. Let this be an end to the matter!

Then someone said, 'I am a servant of Miyan Hafiz Muhammad son of Nur Muhammad of Hajipur. He has sent me on an errand to your Excellence. If leave be granted me, I will lay his request before you.' When the Khwaja told him to speak, he said, 'My master had a dream, in which Your Holiness appeared to him, taught him a verse from the Holy Quran, and told him to keep repeating it. But when he woke up, he was muddled, and could only remember that it went something like "and not saves as a mercy unto all beings". So I have come to find out the exact words of the verse, also when he should recite it, and how many times. Any instructions you may give shall be faithfully carried out.' Then the Khwaja wrote a note in his own blessed hand and gave it to the servant. I give this holy message here, without change or alteration, as a token of piety. It read:

> We have not sent thee, save as a mercy unto all beings (Quran, 21.107). To be repeated 83 times, after the morning prayer, or at any available moment.

Then the servant asked him to provide an amulet for someone else, who was disturbed in heart and troubled in spirit. So the Khwaja wrote out the following verse from the Holy Quran, and gave it to the servant, with instruction that the recipient should hang it round his neck:

> In the name of God, the Compassionate, the Merciful. It is He who sent down tranquility into the hearts of the believers, that they might add faith to their faith. To God belong the hosts of the heavens and the earth; God is All-knowing, All-wise. (Quran, 48.4).

Lesson 7: On Giving Thanks After Death—Unlucky Numbers Ridiculed Thursday, 1st Shaban, A.H. 1311 (8.2.94)

I was granted the supreme blessing of humble attendance upon the holy Khwaja in the middle of the day.

One of the others present in the company asked after someone else, saying, 'I hope all goes well with you?' 'Thanks be to God!' the other replied, but quickly corrected himself, saying, 'That was a mistake, for the time that I shall give thanks will be when I go to Mithankot Sharif.' (What he meant was that the proper time to give thanks was when he was going to be buried there after death).

'My son,' said the Khwaja, 'these words of yours recall the sayings of the greatest Shaikhs. Once, for instance, Shaikh Junaid and some of his companions were talking together. One of them said to another, "I hope you are quite well?" and the other replied, "Thanks be to God!" "My friend," said Shaikh Junaid, "While you are still in the course of your life in this transitory world, what do you know of the manner in which you will leave it? The time to give thanks is when you depart this life with your faith intact, for no one knows what will be the condition of his end."'

The discussion then shifted to the subject of perfect faith, and the Khwaja said, 'When our noble Shaikh, Khwaja Muhammad Aqil, the Lord of the Saints, was asked about perfect faith, he said that it was complete poverty, and gave thanks to God for his own possession of perfect faith.'

Then the musicians came and played. After their performance, the Khwaja gave one of them three rupees, and another ten. The second musician said, 'Lord, the man you gave three rupees to says that three aren't right, and you ought to give him four.' The Khwaja said, 'What a wrong-headed idea this is that simple-minded people have got hold of that three and five are unlucky, because they are odd numbers. They do not realize that the deeds of the great Shaikhs were all odd—that is to say, unique—like 'the acts of the Apostle of God.' Then he smiled, and said, 'Why don't you give back one of your ten rupees, so that you get an odd number too!' everyone burst out laughing, and the man left hurriedly.

Next, the talk was of the way to God. The Khwaja said, 'My own Shaikh used to say that Hazrat Maulana Fakhr-ud-Din of Delhi used to think that the ways which lead one to God are as many as the stars in the sky.'

LESSON 8: THE SAYYIDS AND OTHER GROUPS—ON HINDUISM—
HAFIZ JAMAL AND KHWAJA MUHAMMAD AQIL
SATURDAY, 3RD SHABAN, A.H. 1311 (9.2.94)

I was granted the supreme blessing of humble attendance upon the holy Khwaja in the evening.

The talk turned to the subject of the peoples and groups of mankind. The Khwaja remarked, 'The people of Hindustan, Marwar and Panjab are closely connected with one another, being descended from the Scythians and the ancient local population. But there are four groups who have come from different parts of the world and settled here. These are the Quraish, who have come to our land from Arabia the Holy; the Baloch, who have come from Iran; the Afghans, who are of Khurasanian origin; and the Mughals, whose homeland is in Turkestan.'

At this point someone asked, 'Lord, what people did Khwaja Nizam-ud-Din Badauni of Delhi belong to?' 'He was a Sayyid of Bukharan origin,' replied the Khwaja, 'and was a kinsman of Makhdum Sayyid Jalal-ud-Din Surkh Bukhari of Uch. Seven of the great Sufi saints who belonged to our Chishti line were Sayyids,' he went on. 'Four of these were in Chisht: Khwaja Abu Ahmad Abdal; his son, Khwaja Abu Muhammad; Khwaja Nasr-ud-Din Abu Yusuf; and his son, Khwaja Maudud. Three were in India: Khwaja Muin-ud-Din of Ajmer; Khwaja Qutb-ud-Din Bakhtiyar Kaki; and Khwaja Nizam-ud-Din Badauni of Delhi.'

The same speaker then asked whether Khwaja Imam Hassan Basri was a Sayyid. The Khwaja replied that he was an Arab, but was not descended from Hazrat Ali; it was not known for certain which tribe he belonged to. His interlocutor went on to ask if the Chishti order went back to him. 'Yes,' said the Khwaja, 'he is the pir of pirs, the chief of all Khwajas, and the source of all Shaikhs; for all four orders—Suhrawardi, Qadiri, Naqshbandi, and Chishti—stem from him. He in his turn was the disciple of the Caliph Ali, and received the tokens of successorship directly from his holy hand.'

The discussion then moved on to the religion of the Hindus. The Khwaja said, 'The religion of the Hindus is ancient. Indeed, it is the source and background to all other creeds, and every religion derives from it, for it is the Law of Adam. Every prophet who has succeeded him has evinced hostility towards the religion of the Hindus—which is none other that the religion of Adam—by promulgating the Law he has had revealed to him in his turn, and causing the commandments of his own religion to be put into effect.'

The degrees of sanctity attained by the successors of Hazrat Qibla-e-Alam of Mahar were later discussed, together with the mutual love and affection which prevailed between them. The Khwaja said, 'Hafiz Muhammad Jamal of Multan was the holiest of saints, and between him and our Shaikh, Khwaja Sahib-ur-Rauza, there existed the most perfect love. So profound was the affection which they bore one another that, when our Shaikh was once stricken by illness, and his own treatments proved ineffective in relieving his symptoms, he wrote just this one couplet to Hafiz Jamal:

My soul stands at the brink, so come while I still live:
What use is there in coming after I am dead?

'He sent this by a messenger, who reached Multan at noon. Hafiz Jamal, having performed the midday prayer, was sitting in the mosque, when the messenger handed him the note. After reading it, he told his servant to saddle his horse and bring it to him quickly. He himself set out from where he was in the mosque, without going home and it was not until he reached the harbour of Sher Shah on the bank of the river Chenab—at a distance of some 14 miles from Multan—that his poor servant, out of breath with running, caught up with him and brought him his horse.'

'Notice,' the Khwaja most graciously remarked to me, his humble creature, 'how he hurried off on foot, without delaying even for the time it takes to saddle a horse. He reached our Shaikh the next day, when—simply by their embracing each other—every symptom of his illness was removed. In fact, he looked as if he had never been ill at all.'

'One day,' he continued, 'Hafiz Jamal was sitting with a circle of his friends. Maulavi Gul Muhammad of Ahmadpur, a disciple of our Khwaja Sahib-ur-Rauza, also happened to be present. When he was asked, "Who will be our leader and guardian, friend, after Hazrat Qibla-e-Alam?", the Maulavi replied, "God alone knows!" But Hafiz Jamal said "It will be your pir," meaning that it was to be Khwaja Sahib-ur Rauza.'

LESSON 9: THE CONVERSION OF CHRISTIANS BY KHWAJA FARID'S FAMILY— THE DESIGNATION OF KHWAJA MUHAMMAD AQIL—KHWAJA MUHAMMAD SULAIMAN AND KHWAJA NARUWALA— STORIES OF THE CRAZY HAFIZ JAN MUHAMMAD—NAWAB GHAZI-UD-DIN KHAN. TUESDAY, 7TH SHABAN, A.H. 1311 (12.2.94)

I was granted the supreme blessing of humble attendance upon the holy Khwaja in the evening.

One of the company said, 'A Christian official planned a public highway right in front of the holy tomb of Khwaja Muhammad Aqil. This was his intention by day, but when night intervened, he received a warning in a dream. Next morning he rose and said. "Where is that great saint Khwaja Khuda Bakhsh?" When it was said that he was at Chacharan Sharif, he said, "Arise, that we may humbly go and visit him to ask pardon for our offence!" The official was then granted the honour of a visit to Hazrat Mahbub-e-Ilahi, after which he announced that he had become, with full sincerity of heart, a disciple of the saint.'

'It didn't happen in the way you have told it,' said the Khwaja. 'In fact the story goes like this. He was planning the road in front of the holy enclosure which surrounds the tomb. News of this was brought to Hazrat Mahbub-e-Ilahi, who said, "If he goes through with this, I'll give him a shoe-beating on his head!" Then the Christian official, in complete consternation, refrained from the unholy plan which he had entertained.'

He continued with another anecdote, 'Our Shaikh, Khwaja Fakhr-e-Jahan, once embarked upon a boat in order to voyage to Karachi. Now the boatmen and the servants who accompanied the holy Khwaja to minister to his needs were all his devoted and obedient disciples, zealous in his service and attendance. When the captain of the vessel who was a Christian observed their pious and humble service, and when he beheld the embodiment of pure light in the glorious visage of the saint which is one of the principal outward tokens of sanctity his heart thrilled with faith. He had the saint informed that he was childless, asking that he should pray to God for him to be granted a son. The Khwaja replied that he should be told, "If you enter Islam, I will make myself responsible for your having a son." "I receive a monthly salary of Rs.500 in this position," he said. "If I become a Muslim, this salary will cease to be guaranteed. In fact, I shall be dismissed from my job on the spot." "If they dismiss you," replied my Shaikh, "come and live with me, and I will pay you each month a sum out of my own resources identical with that which you are presently receiving." "Very well, then," he said, "I accept. But I would like to consult my wife about it." So when the Khwaja arrived at Karachi he left him there. When he asked about him on the return journey, he was told that he was dead. The Khwaja expressed his sorrow, and asked how his death had occurred. It was explained that he had said he was going to become a Muslim, but his wife opposed his intention. She reproached him, telling him not to take this step. Finally, when she saw that he was unshaken in his determination to enter Islam, she consulted an English doctor and seemingly administered a fatal poison to her husband, with the result that his soul flew from his body like a bird from its cage.'

'How was his end, Lord?' those present asked. 'Did he die in unbelief or in the faith?' 'His end was praiseworthy,' said the Khwaja, 'for he died in the faith.

'Our pir was indeed a great Shaikh and a mighty Khwaja,' he continued, 'who attained the most exalted status. Miyan Allah Bakhsh of Taunsa has said of him, "It is he who sits by right on the prayer-rug of the Saints of the Way, not us, and not others" And it was indeed as he so justly remarked, for he was in a position to know.'

The Khwaja then spoke of something told him by Hafiz Ghulam Yasin of Chela Wahan, passing on the words of his uncle, Maulavi Ghulam Fakhr-ud-Din, who used to say, 'Khwaja Fakhr-e-Jahan was once going on pilgrimage to the holy tomb of Hazrat Qibla-e-Alam. When he passed by Chela Wahan, I was granted the blessed honour of seeing him. Then I saw that he was immersed in God as the Shaikhs of old used to be. His absorption was indeed real, unlike the counterfeit intentness of others in our time.'

Then the Khwaja said. 'The chosen successor of Hazrat Nur Muhammad Qibla-e-Alam was our Shaikh, Khwaja Muhammad Aqil; and I have several pieces of evidence to prove this was a fact. Firstly, Hazrat Qibla-e-Alam made his own son, Khwaja Nur Hasan, do spiritual homage to Khwaja Muhammad Aqil in his own presence. Although the rest of his deputies were also present, none of the others were so honoured by this special link. The second piece of evidence is that Hazrat Qibla-e-Alam once asked his closest followers if any of them had a vision that day. No one said anything, except for our Khwaja, who said that he had. Then, sitting in private with him, Hazrat Qibla-e-Alam asked him to describe his vision. This he did, in the following terms: "In my vision I saw the Holy Prophet[S.A.W.] with all his noble Companions standing in a certain place, together with all the Pirs of the Order, from Khwaja Hasan Basri to Maulana Fakhr-ud-Din of Delhi. There was also a large tank there, filled to the brim with rose-water mixed with otto. They bathed me in this tank. Then the holy Maulana tied a turban on my head with his own blessed hand, and clothed my body with a robe. Then I woke up. But I still notice the fragrance of that perfume on myself." "Blessed are you!" said Hazrat Qibla-e-Alam, "for this indeed was my desire. Praise be to God that the saint bestowed the turban of successorship upon you with his own blessed hand!"

'In the third place, Hazrat Qibla-e-Alam appointed our Khwaja to administer all his affairs. And fourthly, he was counted among the family of Hazrat Qibla-e-Alam, since his ladies—that is to say, his wives—did not keep purdah before our holy Khwaja, who used to come and go as freely as his own sons. This was a mark of very special closeness, which was not granted to anyone else.

'Sainthood is not restricted to hereditary succession.' he explained. 'Similarly, if the office of prophecy had been purely hereditary there would have been prophets in just a single family, from generation to generation. In fact, precisely the reverse situation applied, as prophets would appear in a place that no one imagined. There is no difference at all in this between the office of a prophet and that of a saint. So in this case Hazrat Qibla-e-Alam bestowed the successorship on the one of his choice, as destiny decreed.

'It is said that the holy martyr, Khwaja Nur-us-Samad begged his father, Hazrat Qibla-e-Alam, two days before the latter's death, graciously to allow him too, some small place in the noble order of the spiritual succession of the Khwajas of Chisht. His father replied, "O my son, now that but two days of my life remain you have remembered. Where were you before? The matter is now out of my hands, but a remedy yet remains. If you adopt this, there is a hope that you may obtain something. The remedy is that you undertake the service of my faqirs as a duty, and count yourself fortunate to be allowed to attend their company."'

He then said, 'Khwaja Muhammad Sulaiman of Taunsa used to say in regard to our Qibla, Khwaja Muhammad Aqil, that if the mantle of prophecy were to come to anyone after the Holy Prophet,[S.A.W.]—who was the seal of the Prophets— would have been granted to him. And Hazrat Qibla-e-Alam used to say of Khwaja Nur Muhammad Naruwala that there was no one like him in the circle of his intimates and disciples. Mark this,' said the Khwaja, graciously addressing me, 'for a pir to say so much about the lofty rank of one of his disciples is a singular mark of his greatness.'

'Khwaja Muhammad Sulaiman of Taunsa also said,' he went on, 'that Khwaja Muhammad Aqil was the intimate companion, continual associate, and close confidant of Hazrat Qibla-e-Alam. Both he and Khwaja Naruwala had general permission not to have to stand waiting when they came, and could go before the saint, whatever he might be doing, and sit down. Hafiz Muhammad Jamal was dependent upon leave being granted. When he came to the door of the saint's chamber, he used to ask permission. If this was given, he would go in and be honoured by audience with the Shaikh. Otherwise he would go away. Holy as he was, he would say about himself, no one used to ask humble disciples like me who was there.'

The Khwaja continued, 'The spiritual influence of Khwaja Muhammad Sulaiman of Taunsa was unrivalled by that of any of the other deputies of Hazrat Qibla-e-Alam. So widespread was it that if we were to collect in one place and count all the direct and indirect disciples of our Qibla, Khwaja Sahib-ur-Rauza (down to my own time), of Khwaja Nur Muhammad Naruwala, of Hafiz Muhammad Jamal, and of Hafiz Ghulam Hasan of Chela Wahan (down to the present), there would be 20,000,000 of them, or at most 25,000,000. This would be less than half the number of those connected; directly, or indirectly, with the spiritual lines of Khwaja Muhammad Sulaiman. His disciples are to be found everywhere, whether we take the area to the west of Taunsa as far as Kandahar and Ghazna, as far as Khurasan and Peshawar to the north, as far as Kashmir to the east, or as far as Hyderabad Deccan in India.'

He then remarked, 'Our Shaikh Khwaja Fakhr-e-Jahan, once visited Ajmer. Five hundred local notables took a vow of allegiance to him there, and allied themselves with his holy Fakhri line.'

Then he said, 'When Khwaja Nur Muhammad Naruwala departed this life to find refuge in God's mercy, his grave in Hajipur was visited by his pir, Hazrat Qibla-e-Alam, who asked the Khwaja's son, Hafiz Muhammad, "Why do you not construct a tomb over your father's grave? For no saint with a tomb that I have seen was greater than he was." "Now that your Excellence has commanded it," Khwaja Hafiz Muhammad obediently replied, "it will be built with all possible speed." Since there were in those days many fervent disciples of the saint to contribute to the expenses, including plenty of men of wealth and substance, a lofty tomb was built and completed. One of those who contributed to the building expenses was Ghazi Khan Daudpotra, of Garhi Ikhtiyar Khan. He was outstanding among the Khwaja's disciples for the extreme fervour of his devotion. This was so great that he is said to have built a lofty mansion in Ghazipur (a village about six miles north of Garhi Ikhtiyar Khan), so that he might sit on its roof and gaze at the glorious prospect of the tomb of his pir.'

After this story was over, this humble creature prostrated himself and asked, 'Lord, how did the holy Khwaja Nur Muhammad get the title of Naruwala?' 'It was the name of a well,' he replied, 'where the Khwaja used to live.'

'Our great Shaikh, Hazrat Sahib-ur-Rauza,' he went on, 'Hazrat Mahbub-e-Ilahi, and our pir, Khwaja Fakhr-e-Jahan, all took it as a duty upon themselves to visit the tomb of Khwaja Nur Muhammad on the occasion of his death-anniversary.'

The discussion then shifted to the subject of staying in the service of one's pir, and of spending time in attendance upon him. The Khwaja explained the practice of former times. 'Six months would be spent by the disciples in the service of their Shaikh, during which they would receive varied instruction and training, practice austerities and mortifications, and be granted spiritual bounties and gifts. The other six months would be spent at home. But, in my opinion, it is better that nine months should be spent with one's Shaikh, and three at home. This is the way to be saved from peril in these times.'

He continued with a story. 'Hafiz Jan Muhammad of Sitpur was a well-known disciple of our Qibla, Hazrat Sahib-ur-Rauza, and had made great spiritual progress. He came once from Sitpur, was granted the privilege of admission to the Shaikh and stayed with him for a while. After some days he decided to return home, and sought leave to depart. The Shaikh told him that it was necessary for him to spend a few more days with him, for he had realized through the light of his inner awareness that manifestations from God were about to be vouchsafed him. But the Hafiz would not accept his advice, and urgently begged to be allowed to leave, like a lover importuning his beloved. "Very well," said the Shaikh, "it you won't stay, then off you go—it's your decision!"

'So, bidding the Shaikh farewell, he set off on his journey. When he reached Wang (a village on the outskirts of Rajanpur, about six miles north-east of Mithankot), he put up for the night with a friend, called Hafiz Ishaq. When day dawned, he performed his ablutions for the morning prayer, advanced to the head of the congregation, and led the people in prayer, in full possession of his faculties. When it came to the final part of the prayer, he jabbered through it, and said, "They did not put it on this side, and they did put it on this side, and they did put it on this side." Then he got up and said something about Hafiz Ishaq which eventually made him die of severe diarrhea. Next he picked up a stout wooden staff and began to beat the people in the mosque. Then he went out into the wilderness. He would block the routes people travelled by and give anyone who came along a severe beating. He was mad for the rest of his days. At the end of his life he used to go about naked, but would beat people rather less than in his earlier years!

'There is another story,' he went on, 'of how some disciples of our Khwaja, Hazrat Mahbub-e-Ilahi, who were involved in a serious trial, came and prostrated themselves before him, begging him to write a letter to a certain official asking him to release those among them who had been detained in prison. "I certainly will not write to the official," said the saint, "but I will write to Hafiz Jan Muhammad the Madman, if you like." They agreed to this suggestion, so the Khwaja wrote the Hafiz a letter, and handed it to them. When they delivered the letter, he read it, kissed it, put it to his eyes, and immediately got up and went off. Some time passed before he returned, when they saw that he had a few carrots on his shoulder. Setting these down before them, he said, "This is all the hospitality I can offer you. I have nothing else to put before you." Then he went straight off to the official, and said to him, "My Shaikh has sent me a letter concerning the release of certain personages. If you will release these prisoners from their captivity, our aim is accomplished. If you do not, they will leave by themselves anyway." "This is not the way things are done," replied the official, "and I certainly will not release them." Then the Hafiz left him and went to the prison, where he told the prisoners, "Break your bonds, and go as you please, for no one will say anything against you!" Believing what he had said, they put his instructions into effect, and went off home. And no one asked why they had done it, or where they were going.

'On this occasion you see,' observed the Khwaja, 'he had become quite rational! There is a similar story of how Maulavi Nur Muhammad Burra of Muhammadpur±—another of the deputies of Hazrat Sahib-ur-Rauza—was one day journeying by boat on the river in order to visit his pir. Now the boat happened to pass close to the bank at a place where there was a dense forest. Suddenly Hafiz Jan Muhammad the madman appeared from the middle of the forest, with his staff on his shoulder. He drew near and asked the Maulavi where he was going. "To attend upon my Shaikh," he replied. "I'll keep you company then," said the madman. Helplessly, the Maulavi invited him into the boat, and he got on and sat down. Everyone was terrified that he would get into a rage, and start fighting and laying about him. But he did not beat anyone.

'They happened to stop for twenty-four hours in the land lying between the rivers. Maulavi Nur Muhammad sent some of his people off to find milk somewhere. They returned empty-handed, saying that the desert folk were disagreeable and rude. Not only had they not given them any milk, but they had told them what they thought of them. Hafiz Jan Muhammad was there, and he became furious when he heard this. "You have been with your Shaikh for all this time," he said to the Maulavi, "and you still can't get hold of a little milk!" There and then he got up and, standing where he was, called out to the buffaloes in the way that herdsmen do at milking or feeding time. Herd upon herd of buffaloes promptly gathered from every direction before the Hafiz. There too came the owners of the buffaloes, stumbling in terror. When they realized what had happened, they all laid their heads at the Hafiz's feet and begged pardon for their transgression. Then they brought so much milk that the Maulavi and those who were with him had more than enough to drink—in fact, they were drinking milk like water.'

At this point somebody asked about the deputies of Hazrat Sahib-ur-Rauza. The Khwaja replied, 'Besides the two whom I have already mentioned (Khwaja Mahbub-e-Ilahi and Maulavi Nur Muhammad), the third was Maulavi Abdullah Thathar of Ahmadpur, the fourth Maulavi Gul Muhammad of the same place, and the fifth Maulavi Sultan Mahmud of Khanbela. But there were also many others.'

One of those in the group then asked, 'Could you tell us about the crazy faqir they used to call Makora, whose nickname was 'Man Man', and who used to spend most of his time in Chacheran Sharif?' 'He was a great faqir,' said the Khwaja, 'and was the disciple of Maulavi Sultan Mahmud of Khanbela.'

Later, princes were discussed, and the Khwaja said, 'Nawab Ghazi-ud-Din Khan of the Deccan gave up the power and position conferred upon him by his royal title, and came to Delhi to serve his pir, Maulana Fakhr-ud-Din. He devoted himself to humble attendance upon the saint, and gave himself up to God. After some time he received his spiritual reward in full—licensed by his pir, he became a perfect saint. He uttered the following verses in praise of his master:

> They rightly call him 'Master of Two Lights'
> For these two lights put heaven in the shade

'The expression, "The Two Lights"', explained the Khwaja, 'refers to the word Nur, or Light, in the names of Hazrat Qibla-e-Alam Nur Muhammad of Mahar and Khwaja Nur Muhammad Naruwala.'

Afterwards, the Khwaja said, 'It is true that the Sabbi allege that the soundness and truth of their religion is upheld by the charter of the Tradition of the Holy Prophet[S.A.W.] addressed to the Caliph Ali, which runs, "You and your Sabbi are in Paradise". But this charter of theirs is not properly applicable to them, since the Sabbi of the Caliph Ali mentioned is the Tradition kept strictly to the Sunna of the Holy Prophet, while also observing the doctrine of concealment, which used to allow them to conceal spiritual mysteries. In complete contrast to them, the Sabbi of the present time have rebelliously turned their backs on the Sunni way, which is the path of the Holy Prophet[S.A.W.] and Lord Ali and have created an evil new religion opposed to that of the Sunni community. They revile the noble Companions of the Prophet,S.A.W. honour and reverence is enjoined by the Quran and by reliable Traditions. How, then, can this sect rightly claim to follow the Lord Ali? And what right have they to cite this Tradition as a charter?'

'This heresy,' he went on, 'has now become exceedingly prevalent in our country. This was certainly not the case in former times, when even the wandering qalandars, the dervishes who shaved themselves like yogis, and the oddly dressed followers of Lal Shahbaz used to be proper Sufis and Sunnis. None of them used to revile the Companions of the ProphetS.A.W.. Even now there are some faqirs of this type in India, who follow the true way and possess right beliefs.

'When I went to Multan,' he continued, 'the Gardezi Sayyids came to meet me. I have seen it recorded in one of the Gardezis' books that their original forebear, Sayyid Yusuf Gardezi, was a direct disciple of Hazrat Abu Yazid Bistami.'

Lesson 10: Miracles of Shaikh Abdul Qadir Gilani—A Miracle of Shaikh Abul Abbas of Amul—Against the Kharijites
Saturday, 11th Shaban, 1311 (16.2.94)

I was granted the supreme blessing of humble attendance upon the holy Khwaja in the evening.

The glories and miracles of that greatest of saints, Shaikh Abdul Qadir Gilani, were being discussed. One of those present said, 'Lord, it is commonly held that the Shaikh's holy foot has rested upon the neck of every saint. Could you tell us more about this?'

The Khwaja explained, 'One day the Shaikh was sitting on a chair, preaching a sermon, when a miraculous vision came to him from the unseen world. The Holy ProphetSAW appeared in their glory, followed by the angels and cherubim. A call came from God, saying, "O Abdul Qadir, I have placed all the saints beneath your foot. Call them, and make them pass beneath it!" Then he said "Let this foot of mine rest upon the neck of each of God's saints!" As soon as they heard this divinely inspired call, all the saints of the highest ranks who were then living on the earth, whether near or far, and whether they were equal in dignity to Shaikh Abdul Qadir or of lesser degree (but had still reached the ultimate stages of spiritual evolution), were exalted by passing eagerly and obediently beneath the blessed foot of the saint. The saints of earlier and later ages, and neophytes and those who had not reached the final stages of the mystical way, were not included in this command, which was exclusively addressed to those perfect saints who were alive at the same time as the Shaikh. More than one hundred of these very great saints were actually present in the congregation to which he was addressing his sermon, and those were all honoured by lowering their necks beneath the blessed foot of

Shaikh Abdul Qadir. The one who hastened to be the first to receive this honour was that renowned and most perfect saint, Shaikh Ali Hitti.

'The Saints of the Neck,' he continued, 'fall into two categories, the present and the absent. The present had the Shaikh's foot visibly placed upon their necks for everyone, of whatever degree, to see, whereas the absent had his foot set upon their necks by inner faith, invisible to anyone there other than the obedient saint himself. Shaikh Abu Madyan Maghribi, for instance—the pir of Shaikh Muhyud Din ibn ul Arabi—was sitting at home in the Maghrib, enjoying himself with his companions, when he suddenly bowed his neck and said, "We have heard and obeyed the command of God!" His friends, who had been in that company, later asked him in private about the state of rapture which had overcome him. The Shaikh replied, "Today God has spoken to Shaikh Abdul Qadir Gilani and authorised him to say, 'Let this foot of mine rest upon the neck of each of God's saints!' All the saint of the age have humbled themselves and placed their necks beneath his blessed foot. So I, too, have demonstrated my submission to God's command by placing my neck beneath his foot.'

Somebody asked at this point whether Khwaja Muin ud-Din of Ajmer was one of the 'Saints of the Neck.' The Khwaja answered by saying, 'I think he would have been 18 years old at the time, and hence at the beginning of his spiritual progress. But it certainly would not be surprising if his pir Shaikh Usman Haruni, were to have been one. Even if he was not, then his pir, Haji Sharif Zindani, most assuredly would have been.'

He went on, 'One of the titles of the Shaikh was "the Preacher", because he used to preach a sermon every Friday. While preaching, he used to be subject to miraculous visions. About 70,000 people used to attend his sermons. One of the saint's greatest miracles was that those who were far away used to hear and understand every word of his sermons just as clearly as those who were placed near him. And whenever he was speaking of the awesome majesty of Almighty God, or expounding some mystery of divine love, one hundred of those in the congregation would fall martyr to the pangs of fear or love, and hasten from this transitory world to their permanent abode.

'One day,' he continued, 'he was sitting preaching. Shaikh Ali Hitti was sitting at the foot of his throne, when he was suddenly overcome by sleep. Shaikh Abdul Qadir descended from his throne to stand with the greatest respect before Shaikh Ali until the latter awoke. When he asked him what he had seen in his dream, Shaikh Ali replied, "I was granted the blessed honour of beholding the Holy Prophet,[A.S]. "It was because of this," said Shaikh Abdul Qadir, "that I stood in deep respect before you."'

At this point the Khwaja paused to comment on how the fact that one of them saw the Holy Prophet[S.A.W.] in a dream, the other while awake, pointed to the difference between them, and to the higher rank of Shaikh Abdul Qadir.

He went on with another story. 'One day, a man called Abul Maali was sitting in the congregation before Shaikh Abdul Qadir, when he was overtaken by an urgent call of nature. He controlled himself so violently that his senses raced, a blackness came before his eyes, and he turned a terrible colour. He was unable to go outside due to the great crowd of people, so he looked in the direction of the Shaikh, only to see that a form exactly like that of the Shaikh had emerged from him. One of the two forms went on preaching, while the other came down from the throne to stand before the desperate man, and cast the sleeve of its gown over his face. No one except for him observed any of this. Then he found himself in a great desert through which there ran a stream of flowing water, with a tree on its bank. Abul Maali had with him a bunch of keys tied to the corner of his hand-kerchief. These he hung on a branch of that tree, before setting about satisfying his need. After he had relieved himself, he performed his ablutions and offered a double prayer of thanksgiving for his release from his terrible plight. He complet-ed his prayer and asked for God's blessing. Then the Shaikhs removed his sleeve from his face, and he found himself back in the congregation, in just the same place as before, with the moisture on his body showing that he had performed his ablutions a short while beforehand.'

Some time later, this same Abul Maali was traveling in the direction of Mo-sul, when one day he happened to reach the desert where he had relieved himself and performed his ablutions. Recognizing the landmarks, he went to the tree on which he had tied his handkerchief with the keys on. He found it still hanging there, so he united the handkerchief and went on his way. On his return, he was granted the privilege of attendance upon the Shaikh. He wanted to tell him what had happened, but the Shaikh murmured in his ear, 'I know about the story of the handkerchief. Don't tell anyone else about it.'

The Khwaja then told another story. 'There was once a merchant who was a disciple of Shaikh Hammad Dabbas, a pir in Shaikh Abdul Qadir's circle. Now, when he had packed up his merchandise and was about to set off on a trip, it was that merchant's habit to go to his pir, Shaikh Hammad, and ask for his blessings on the profitability of his undertakings. His choice of which country to go to was always determined by the Shaikh's instructions, and when he returned, he would regularly make the Shaikh an offering of a fixed portion of his profit. Once he went to the Shaikh, and said, "Lord, I have got my merchandise ready. Please grant your blessing, that, I may return safe and successful. I will go to any coun-try that you may suggest." "On this occasion," the Shaikh replied, "it is decreed by fate that, if you go to such-and-such a country, you will amass a considerable profit; but, when you reach a certain place on your return journey, robbers will not only plunder your wealth, but will kill you too."

'Then the unhappy merchant left Shaikh Hammad, and went to Shaikh Abdul Qadir, repeating everything to him. Shaikh Abdul Qadir replied. "This time I will stand as your guarantor. Off you go, for you will leave safely and return whole." So he went off to that country. When he arrived, he sold his goods and made a substantial profit. On his return journey, he arrived at the place mentioned by Shaikh Hammad. That night he had a dream, that he was in a caravan which was being plundered by robbers, that the robbers were killing the people in the caravan, and that they slew him, too, with swords. When he awoke in terror from this nightmare, he found that there was a cut in the skin on his throat. But it was not a serious wound; and his goods, too, were safe. When he went and told Shaikh Hammad what had happened, he said, "This change was brought about by Shaikh Abdul Qadir, who converted into a dream your murder and robbery, which were destined to happen in reality."'

When this story was over, one of the holy Khwaja's closest and most favoured disciples, Fazl-ul-Haq, the son of Khwaja Nasir Bakhsh Mangherwi of Mahar, said 'Once my father wrote a letter to Hazrat Mahbub-e-Ilahi, in which he included these verses:

> The saints in part possess the power of God:
> They can deflect an arrow in its flight.

Hazrat Mahbub-e-Ilahi later said that the verse applied to Shaikh Abdul Qadir.'

To this the Khwaja said, 'My Shaikh, Khwaja Fakhr-e-Jahan, told me that Maulavi Nur Muhammad Burra once asked Hazrat Qibla-e-Alam about the meaning of these verses. "I am no mullah, friend," he replied, "you are the learned one. But what I think it means is that, in his intentions, a saint does not seek to oppose destiny, for what a saint desires is indeed destiny. Destiny is identical with his desire, since his every word and deed is uttered and performed by God. And all that is issued and manifested from God constitutes destiny."

Then he said, 'Shaikh Abdul Abbas the "Butcher" of Amul was a mighty Shaikh, whose supreme sanctity is universally admitted. ("Universally admitted supreme sanctity"—also known as "totally supreme sanctity"—is that which is confirmed by all the saints of the time: such supreme saints are few.) He used to tell the disciples and friends who came to attend upon him, "My friends, do not occupy yourselves with any prayers or devotions other than those enjoined by God or by the example of the Prophet.[S.A.W.] Rather enjoy yourselves, for this butcher has passed beyond the stage of worship. He has no need of it for himself, and every act of worship he now performs, he does for you.'"

'The story is told,' he went on, 'that one day a boy was leading a heavily laden camel by its halter through the bazaar in Amul. The camel chanced to slip and break its leg. The boy gave a cry, and wept bitterly. Now Shaikh Abdul Abbas was there. Taking pity on his tears, he prayed, "O God, either mend the camel's leg, or cease to afflict this butcher's heart with the boy's crying!" The camel instantly got up and moved quickly away.'

The discussion then turned to the abomination of Shias and its adherents. (This discussion went on for a long time, and only a brief summary has been provided.)

The Khwaja said, 'The doctrines of the Shia and the Kharijiya are false, and all the sects which belong to these two groups have turned away from the true path. A Shia is one who loves the Caliph Ali, and thinks of the other noble Caliphs as detestable enemies, to be reviled and insulted. A Khariji is one who reviles and insults all the noble Caliph other than Abu Bakr and Umar, the reason being that the Kharijis say that the Sunna of the Prophet[S.A.W.] was in force only up to the period of their Caliphate, and was abrogated and discontinued in the time of the other Righteous Caliphs: hence the coming to pass amongst them of wars and dissension, due to selfish pride. But I seek refuge with God from this false faith of theirs! The Kharijis are guilty of calumny and slander, because all the noble Caliphs acted in accordance with the Sunna of the Holy Prophet.[S.A.W.] The fighting and dissension came about through the desire to wage holy war for the truth, not through pride and selfishness; because, when they saw that one was right, the rest abandoned their opposition and followed him in that matter.'

Then somebody said that he had once had an argument with a Shia, and asked him why he reviled the noble Caliphs. 'If a rival saint were to fight with your pir,' he said, 'you might not join in the fight, but you would certainly hate and curse him.'

The Khwaja then said, 'I think this point can be effectively disposed of by the following argument. The accursedness of Satan is authoritatively laid down. But if anyone does not curse Satan at any point his life, this does not count against him as a sin, nor will he be charged with not having done so on the day of Resurrection; for we are not ordered to curse anyone. So why do they curse and revile the noble caliphs, whose honour and glory has been established by unambiguous verses in the holy Quran, and by authentic traditions? Those who revile the noble companions of the Prophet are themselves companions of hell-fire, who will be afflicted with the direst torments on the Day of Judgment. Given this, one should not say anything against a Shaikh who is an enemy and opponent of one's own shaikh. What do those who are not themselves saints know about the controversies of Shaikhs anyway? So a man should restrain his tongue from reviling and taunting not only the noble companions, but also indeed the saints, who have been granted the rank of near approach to God. He should not let such thoughts even enter his heart, for by this dangerous step alone—without uttering anything with his tongue—a faqir's faith may be destroyed completely. And may God preserve us from that!'

LESSON 11: ON THE EXALTATION OF ONE'S OWN PIR
WEDNESDAY, 12TH RAMAZAN 1311 A.H. (20.3.94)

I was granted the supreme blessing of humble attendance upon the holy Khwaja in the evening.

The relative superiority of different shaikhs was being discussed, when the Khwaja said, 'A saint may announce, on the basis of a mystical revelation, that such-and-such a saint is superior to all others. But there is no need to follow his announcement and to suppose that that saint is uniquely superior in sanctity; for it is a universal rule that one's own shaikh and the preceding shaikhs of his line always seem superior to others, in any visionary revelation.'

Here the Khwaja told the following story. Shaikh Rukn ud-Din Ala-ud-Daula Simnani said that, 'When he established the ties of his order with the Kubrawi order, he was asked, "Why did you not take your oath of spiritual allegiance in the Taifuri order of Abu Yazid Bistami, than whom no greater shaikh has been born on the face of the earth?" He replied, "Because one sensed, and became unconscious. In that state I saw the veil lifted from the Kaaba, and a heaven appeared beyond this heaven. And there was a star in that heaven, very brilliant and shining like the sun. Then I heard the voice of one weeping, saying to me, "Do you know who this brilliant light comes from?" "No, I do not," he replied. Then the voice said, "It is part of the light of Abu Yazid Bistami." Then that heaven vanished, and another heaven appeared. This was as brilliant as the star in the first heaven, and in it there was a star of even greater radiance. Then somebody spoke, and asked him. "Do you know who this light comes from?" "No, I do not," he replied. Then he said, "This brilliant light is part of the light of the Kubrawi Shaikh Majid-ud-Din of Baghdad."'

The Khwaja commented, 'Although the ties of Shaikh Rukn ud-Din's order were fated to be fixed with the Kubrawi order, he was still thus impelled to acknowledge the superiority of the saint he had chosen through this vision.'

He continued on the same theme, 'Shaikh Abdul Haq Muhaddis of Delhi has written of how Shaikh Abdul Wahhab Muttaqi used to tell of the meeting with the Holy Prophet[S.A.W.] which he was vouchsafed one night. "Who in your community is the greatest saint at the present time?" he asked and the Holy Prophet[S.A.W.] answered, "It is Shaikh Ali Muttaqi." "Who is the best after him?" he asked, and the Holy Prophet answered, "It is Shaikh Tahir Bora." Now Shaikh Ali Muttaqi was the pir of Shaikh Abdul Wahhab, and Shaikh Tahir Bora was his brother's pir!"

Again on the same subject, the Khwaja said, 'Shah Waliullah Muhaddis of Delhi said of the revelations granted to him that they were so exact that the circumstances of the whole earth and its creatures were as open to him as the lines on his hand, in fact, he could see them even more clearly than this. Because of one revelation he had seen, he said that Hazrat Shah Habibullah, known as Mirza Jan-e-Janan, was greater than all other saints notwithstanding the fact that there were certainly many other great saints in existence at the time, including Hazrat Maulana Fakhr-ud-Din of Delhi who was looked up to by all the great Shaikhs of those days, and many others too. But he still said that Mirza Jan-e-Janan was superior to all these, and the reason was that Shah Waliullah and Mirza Jan-e-Janan belonged to the same order!'

LESSON 12: APPROVAL OF LESSONS 4–7—
FANTASTIC TALES OF MAKHDUM JAHANIYAN REFUTED
FRIDAY, 21ST RAMAZAN, A.H. 1311 (29.3.94)

I was granted the supreme blessing of humble attendance upon the holy Khwaja in the evening.

I humbly presented the holy Khwaja with all that I had so far recorded and written of his saintly teachings, from lesson 4–7. He told all those present to go out. When they had all left, he told me to read. Following his instruction, I read out all I had written, while the Khwaja listened to each word, making corrections in one or two places. After the reading was finished, he granted me permission to record his precious utterances, as if awarding me the key to a casket of jewels. He also promised that he would listen to every section which I composed and check it, so that I could then include it in my book. He also returned the pages which I had previously presented to him (as mentioned in Lesson 4), which he had checked. Praise be to God for his graciousness!

This was the end of my private audience, and the company re-assembled. The question of contradictions between what is said in different books came up and the Khwaja said, 'In *Jawahir-e-Jalali* and the *Jami-ul-Ulum*, which are both books containing the sayings of Sayyid Jalal-ud-Din Makhdum Jahaniyan of Uch, a Khariji is defined as one who hates and reviles the Caliph Ali, but loves and accepts the other three Caliphs as rightly guided. Now this definition stands in stark contradiction to all previous books and early traditions. Still, the author does say that every word had been diligently gone over and checked with the Makhdum several times. So it may well have been that this was the traditional definition which had been passed on to the Makhdum. Since the matter is one of the handing down of traditions, there are various ways in which it could be explained.

'There is a book called the *Travels of Makhdum Jahaniyan*,' he continued, 'which is totally unjust to the Makhdum. The entire contents of the book are a complete tissue of lies. One of the fabrications in this collection of untruths occurs when the author writes that the Makhdum, during his travels in the western lands, came to a city called Constantinople, where he saw 100,000 bazaars, each with 100,000 shops. This is a downright lie, for I have never heard of a city of this name and description called Constantinople other than the presently flourishing and famous city of Istanbul. Nor is any other city of this name and description in the Western lands mentioned in any work of history. Now in the Constantinople which is at present the capital of the Ottoman Empire there are at most 200,000 houses, so one can hardly talk in terms of 100,000 bazaars. Of course, the description would be quite in order if there were a city of this name and description in the unseen world!

'A second falsehood is perpetrated by the author of the *Travels*, when he writes that once, during his journeys, Makhdum Jahaniyan reached the end of the world and saw that the sky was touching the earth. So he hung his cloak on the edge of the sky and busied himself with an urgent task. When he looked up, he saw that his cloak was no longer there. So he stood where he was for eight watches, until that bit of sky on which he had hung his cloak came back. Then he took back his cloak and departed.

'Now this is arrant nonsense. In the first place, the highest heaven surrounds the sphere of the throne, the sphere of the throne surrounds the heavenly spheres in their concentric order, and the heavenly spheres surround the earthly spheres of fire, air, water and earth. So the distance between the earth and the sky, from all sides of the earth, is equivalent to a journey of 500 years according to the cosmologists, while the natural scientists put it at 500,000 miles. So how can the sky touch the earth? And if we accept that the sky has an 'edge', how can it be maintained that it is a perfect sphere with no ups and downs or bumps in it?

'In the second place, the sky moves millions of miles in a few seconds. We all know that there are 60 seconds in a minute and 60 minutes in an hour, and that 12 hours make 4 watches. So if we think of one part of the sky as a marker, that imaginary mark will have passed by many times in eight watches. It must, therefore, be incorrect to say that it took eight watches for the bit of sky on which the cloak was hung to come back.'

LESSON 13: AGAINST LEAVING ONE'S PIR ON A WEDNESDAY—A PIR'S ANGER
TUESDAY, 3RD SHAWWAL, A.H. 1311 (10.4.94)

I was granted the supreme blessing of humble attendance upon the holy Khwaja in the afternoon.

The Khwaja said, 'I have summoned you so that you can put whatever question you have during this hour, before you take your leave of me to go home before sunset this evening. For tomorrow is Wednesday, and it is forbidden to leave one's pir on a Wednesday.' Then he granted me a private audience, and I read out some questions to him which I had written down on a piece of paper. Each of these he answered with perfect insight.

'Lord,' I then said, 'I, your lowly disciple, am so in awe of your Holiness that my body is sometimes overcome by trembling, because I am afraid that this poor creature of yours may be unable to help doing something unseemly, which may offend the sainted Khwaja.' The Khwaja smiled, and answered with the greatest kindness. 'A pir is never annoyed with his disciple. If he is, then it is for the latter's benefit. For a pir is the bridesmaid of his disciple, and the bridesmaid's task is to prepare the bride properly, and to adorn her in every way that she wishes.'

He went on to repeat the story from the *Fawaid-ul-Fuad* of how Khwaja Nizam ud Din Badauni of Delhi said, 'I was reading the *Awarif-ul-Marif* with my pir one day. Because the manuscript was not written in a good or clear hand, my holy Shaikh was puzzled and uncertain about several minor points. Unthinkingly, I let fall the words, "Shaikh Najib ud Din has a reliable copy, written in a much clearer hand than this one." My Shaikh was annoyed, and said, "A mere faqir does not have the power to correct mistakes, or to distinguish the authentic from the apocryphal!" Then he brusquely sent me away, and did not allow me to come near him. In this dreadful state I spent several days. The close associates of my pir interceded with him for me, but without producing any softening of his attitude. Finally, I made up my mind to hurl myself into a well, since death were better than living like this. Then my very good friend, Khwaja Nizam ud Din, the Shaikh's son, interceded successfully with his father, who immediately sent for me and was prodigal with his favour, saying,

> The appearance of the elder's wrath is not without its aim:
> The dust that lies on heaven's face is proof of love's approach, for a pir is the bridesmaid of his disciple.'

Then the sun went down, and it was time for the sunset prayer. 'Now it is Wednesday,' said the Khwaja. 'Actually,' I said, 'I have decided to go after Wednesday is passed.' 'Praise be to God!' he replied.

What blessings I was vouchsafed in this private audience!

Lesson 14: The Festival at Mithankot: The Prophet's Footprint is Venerated
Saturday, 11th Zil Hijja, A.H. 1311 (16.6.94)

I was granted the supreme blessing of humble attendance upon the holy Khwaja in the afternoon.

The Khwaja was seated in the courtyard of the mosque which lies beside the glorious tomb at Mithankot. A great press of people, some sitting and others standing, were in a ring around him, falling over each other in their eagerness to see and to kiss the feet of the holy saint. The rush was, in fact, so great that it was scarcely possible to find a place in which to set one's feet; for it was the occasion of Khwaja Mahbub-e-Ilahi's anniversary festival.

Then the attendants of the tomb placed the reliquary chest containing the footprint of the Holy Prophet[S.A.W.] on a charpoy-bed before the Khwaja, who immediately told the servant who had been given the task of waving his fan to desist. He obeyed, and stopped fanning. Since the summer heat was fierce and there was no breeze that day—let alone the fact that the people were crowding densely round him—perspiration flowed so freely from the blessed body of the Khwaja that his clothes became drenched, while the rest dripped on to the ground. The Khwaja's body turned such a delicate colour that it might—albeit with disrespect—be compared to the petals of the rose. In spite of all this, he kept his head lowered on his bosom as a humble token of respect, in a position of majestic repose.

Finally, after a great many poems had been sung, the attendants took out from its casket the piece of stone on which the holy footprint was impressed, and brought it to the Khwaja, who bowed his head right down over it. Then, touching the holy footprint with the edge of his shawl, he rubbed its sacred impression over his eyes. After this, everyone venerated the relic.

Lesson 15: In Praise of Ice—Against Leaving on a Wednesday— The Disobedience of Haji Abdul Khair
Wednesday, 15th Zil Hijja, A.H. 1311 (19.6.94)

I was granted the supreme blessing of humble attendance upon holy Khwaja in the evening.

'Two things in this world are tokens of Paradise:' said the Khwaja, 'fans and ice in the hot season!' He continued, 'The British have dug tanks, into which a device has been inserted to make their water just like ice, so that you cannot tell the difference. I have myself seen these tanks in Lahore, Amritsar and Delhi, and have drunk water from them.'

Then someone said, 'Lord, I have got a poisoned spot on the end of my finger, which causes me great pain, and gives me no rest by day or night.' The Khwaja recited some verses from the Holy Quran and blew on his finger, then recommended bleeding as the best treatment. Somebody else who was there suggested cutting the cephalic vein in the arm. 'No,' said the Khwaja, 'the cephalic vein helps the head, and what he needs to do is to bleed a vein which helps the hand.'

Then he said, 'Ice possesses this great power, that if a piece is placed on a septic spot of any kind and is replaced by another, if necessary, when it melts then, by God's grace, the poison is dissolved, and no trace of the spot remains. This is a tried and true remedy.'

Miyan Ghaus Bakhsh then said, 'Lord, your servant plans to go home. I will leave in the morning.' 'Don't go tomorrow,' said the Khwaja, 'because tomorrow is Wednesday. And there is that story of how our Shaikh, Hazrat Sahib-ur-Rauza, used to say to anyone asking this leave to depart on that day, "Dear son, do you desire never to return to me?"'

He continued with another anecdote. 'A disciple asked Hazrat Qibla-e-Alam for leave to depart on a Wednesday. "Don't go today," he said, "because it is forbidden to take leave of one's Shaikh on a Wednesday." But he insisted on going so pathetically, offering all sorts of reasons, that he was finally granted permission to depart, and off he went. On the way he happened to fall into the hands of robbers, who ripped off his clothes and beat him up. Naked and weeping, he returned to the Shaikh, and told him what had happened on the way. "My dear fellow," said the saint, "did I not tell you not to go today? In spite of this you would not stay and off you went. What you have experienced is all part of the unluckiness and inauspiciousness of a Wednesday subsequently in order to get rid of the mistaken idea that Wednesday has no power to harm people. For it derives its power from Almighty God, and it is to this delegated authority that its inauspiciousness is to be attributed."

The failure of disciples to pay due regard to their pir and to be properly conscious of their dependence upon him was then discussed, and the Khwaja said, 'A certain Haji Abul Khair of Hajipur Sharif was returning home from his Pilgrimage to Mecca. On his way back he was seized somewhere near Rojhan by some mazaris, who were robbers and footpads. They tore the clothes from his body, robbed him of the holy relics from Mecca and Medina he was carrying, and left him naked. In this wretched state of nakedness he reached our Qibla, Hazrat Sahib-ur-Rauza, in Mithankot Sharif. Hiding behind the wall, he stood near the door of the great house inside which the saint was sitting. He was stretching up to look inside the house, then getting down again, when our Qibla recognized him, and asked if he was Haji Abul Khair. A groan escaped him, and he wept bitterly. A sheet was thrown to him, and with this wrapped around him he entered the house, and was allowed to kiss the feet of the Shaikh. He related everything that had befallen him. The Shaikh was overcome by pity for his sorry state, and told a servant to bring a special bundle of his own clothes. First he took out a pair of loose trousers from the bundle and, laying then on his blessed hands, told him to put them on. He did so, and by the mere act of putting them on, his expression changed and he had a marvellous inner vision. Then the Shaikh laid a shirt on his blessed hand and told him to put that on. When he did so, his ecstasy was increased. Then he was given a cap, and when he put this on his head, his rapture reached a still more excited pitch, and he was transported into the world of the unseen. Then the saint said, "Abul Khair, you have been separated from your family for a long time. Those left behind must be grieving for you, and you must be longing to see them. It is time you went home now." So he left immediately.

'Each day his repute grew more and more intense, and his every moment was spent in the most profound ecstasy. Great numbers of people kept coming to him and when one lot left, another group would attach themselves to him. Wherever he was, a great throng of people would crowd around him. Anyway, one day our Qibla arrived, on his return from a visit to the holy festival of Khwaja Naruwala. Seeing him from afar, everyone came and prostrated themselves at his blessed feet. Now Haji Abul Khair, who ought to have been the first to come and perform the ceremonies of submission to his pir, was instead the last. In fact, he stayed sitting where he was. Still worse, the dangerous idea entered his head that "He may be a Shaikh, but so am I." No sooner had he entertained this perilous notion than the saint approached him. Although he still did not get up, our Qibla put his blessed hand on his head and rubbed it, saying, "All is well, Haji ji." With that simple movement of the saint's hand, his state was brought back to normal, and he became as he had been before being overtaken by rapture.'

LESSON 16: THE FESTIVAL AT MITHANKOT— PEOPLE SEEK THE KHWAJA'S BLESSING
WEDNESDAY, 15TH ZIL HIJJA A.H. 1311 (20.6.94)

I was granted the supreme blessing of humble attendance upon the holy Khwaja in the afternoon.

The Khwaja was sitting in the courtyard of the mosque, facing the holy tomb. There was a huge throng of people gathered there. Each would come up in turn to make his personal request.

One of these prostrated himself and said, 'Lord, please add something in your own blessed hand to this holy scroll of the saints written by the illustrious Shaikh, that I may keep this too as a relic to be venerated.' The Khwaja then wrote the following words. 'O God, abasing himself in the dust on the path of those who are stricken with love for You, Your humble creature Ghulam Farid asks that he be granted his brother's happy end.' Then another person also got the Khwaja to write the same words on his copy of the holy scroll.

Later, someone else laid a dish filled with water before the Khwaja. Weeping and groaning, he said that he suffered from a chronic illness, and asked the Khwaja to recite something over the water, so that he might drink it as the best remedy for his affliction. So the Khwaja recited something over the water, breathed on it, and gave it to him.

Afterwards, since many people were coming up and sorely troubling the Khwaja by their kissing of his hands and feet, he told everyone to stay in their places, while he recited a general prayer for them all. Then he raised his hands to invoke God's blessing, and prayed aloud for a long time.

LESSON 17: THE KHWAJA'S DEVOTIONS AT MITHANKOT
FRIDAY, 17TH ZIL HIJJA, A.H. 1311 (21.6.94)

I was granted the supreme blessing of humble attendance upon the holy Khwaja at sunset.

The Khwaja was sitting in the courtyard on the north side of the holy tomb. Its surface was constructed of baked bricks, made blisteringly hot by the heat of the sun. He was occupied with his private devotions, and everybody sat absolutely quiet and silent.

At that moment Nawab Ghulam Dastgir Khan of the Deccan arrived. Notable for his sincere devotion to the Khwajas of the holy Chishti order, he was in this part of the world at the time on account of some important business, and had decided to offer his humble respects to the Khwaja. He kissed the ground, and touched the Khwaja's blessed foot with his forehead, before sitting down.

The Khwaja had then just finished performing the sunset prayer, and had returned to his customary private devotions. I record here what I managed to hear of these: the Sura of the Tidings (Quran 78) five times; the Fatiha (Quran ,1) five times; Sura of Sincere Religion (Quran 112) sixteen times all accompanied by the invocation of the name of God. Then he recited for a while in a low voice, so that it was impossible to tell what it was. He then started to recite in a loud voice the Fatiha once, followed by the Verse of the Throne once (Quran 2.255) up to the word Khalidan at the end of verse 257—both accompanied by the name of God and the Sura of Sincere Religion several times. While he was busy with these regular devotions, he asked for water. A servant went and brought it very quickly, and he drank it. After finishing his devotions he arose and went into the holy tomb, without raising his hands to invoke God's blessing. An hour later he emerged from the tomb and went to his house.

LESSON 18: DEATH OF SHAIKH MARUF KARKHI—THE FOUR KINDS OF PRIDE— AGAINST CONDEMNING MINOR MISPRONUNCIATIONS IN THE PRAYER
SUNDAY, 19TH ZIL HIJJA, A.H. 1311 (23.6.94)

I was granted the supreme blessing of humble attendance upon the holy Khwaja in the evening.

The lofty moral qualities of the holy company of saints were being discussed. The Khwaja said, 'Shaikh Maruf Karkhi lived at a time of Holy War, when the fight against unbelievers and adherents of false religions was in progress. Yet he himself was so broad in his outlook that he told his friends, when he was about to die, "After my death everyone—whether Muslim, Jew, Christian, Magian or of any other religion—will put forward the claim, 'This Shaikh was of our religion.' I want you, my friends, to understand that anyone who is able to take up my bier can be sure that I was of his religion, and may perform its last rites after he has done so." Now when the saint died and was received into the mercy of God, the very thing which he had foretold came to pass, that is, Muslims, Jews, Christians, and Magians, each claimed that he was one of them. Then the Caliph of Baghdad arrived, and said, "I will decide this matter in accordance with the words of the holy Shaikh, and the group which is able to take up his bier is right." Finally the Muslims took it up, whereupon all the other claimants withdrew their claims and handed it into the keeping of the Muslims.'

He than continued, 'The saint's death came about in the following fashion. One day he had gone to see his pir, the holy Imam Musa Riza. So dense were the crowds of people there that he fell to be martyred by being trampled beneath their feet.'

Then the talk turned to the overweening pride that stems from the possession of great learning. 'Pride can be of four kinds:' said the Khwaja, 'pride of the self, pride of knowledge, pride of lineage, and pride of wealth. If you suffer from pride of the self and behave in accordance with the verse, "Will you bid others to piety and forget yourselves?" (Quran, 2.44), then look at Satan. If you suffer from pride of knowledge, once more look at Satan, and recall the eternal damnation which befell Balaam son of Baur. If you suffer from pride of lineage, look at the fate of the son of Noah. And if you suffer from pride of wealth, look at Pharaoh, Shaddad, Nimrod, and the others, and what happened to them!"

One of those present in the company then said, 'Lord, there is a certain religious scholar who says that it is unlawful for anyone to offer prayer if he does not pronounce the words of the Holy Quran in strict accordance with the rules of recitation—as, for instance, happens when the word Al-Hamd is pronounced with the soft 'h', instead of the hard 'h'.'

'Don't you remember the title story?' said the Khwaja, 'it tells, how the Holy Prophet^{S.A.W.} said of Bilal that he pronounced 's' as 'sh'? And there is also the story of Khwaja Habib Ajami, the greatest successor of Khwaja Imam Hasan Basri. He was once acting as leader of the prayer, and was not pronouncing the Holy Quran in accordance with the rules of recitation. When someone objected, saying he had not recited properly, Khwaja Habib retorted, "You have set the outside of the Holy Quran in order, we the inside."'

He continued, pursuing the same theme, 'There were many learned religious scholars in the happy days of our Qibla, Hazrat Mahbub-e-Ilahi, but one of them raised this kind of pettifogging objection. Or course, the saint was himself such an expert that none of his contemporaries dared to argue points of Law against him. All the same, he would sometimes knowingly pray behind someone who not only was ignorant of the rules of recitation, but did not even know the proper letters, words and pauses. Yet he would not say anything about the way he pronounced the prayer. Nowadays, of course, these mullahs get up and make all sorts of petty points and niggling objection!"

Lesson 19: Rukn ud-Din Reproved—The Khwaja Raises a Storm
Tuesday, 27th Zil Hijja, A.H. 311 (2.7.94)

I was granted the supreme privilege of humble attendance upon the holy Khwaja in the evening.

The Khwaja was reclining somewhat upon his seat, in order to rest. He had his rosary in his hand, and was reciting a private devotion. He then sat up and asked, 'Who has just sat down—was it Rukn ud Din?' When one of his servants told him that it was, he graciously addressed me, saying, 'Perhaps you were here all the time?' 'Yes, Lord, I was,' I answered respectfully.

Here it needs to be realized that everyone had gone home at the end of the festival of Khwaja Mahbub-e-Ilahi, leaving only a few of his close servants to attend upon the holy Khwaja. When he then left Mithankot for Chacharan, even those disciples who remained had taken their leave and departed. Only this poor creature was left. But for two or three days I had been unable, on account of some business I had, to come and have the honour of attendance upon the Khwaja. So he thought that maybe I had gone too. That was why he asked if it was me who was there. His question also implied a reproof, for if I had been there all the time, why had I not come to see him again, since the most direct route to union with God is through attendance upon one's Shaikh. But the Khwaja's reproof was only implicit, so that I—while aware of its import—was not publicly charged with lack of respect towards him.

Then he turned to the north, and said, 'There is a cloud over there. And there was indeed a small cloud on the horizon in that quarter. When the Khwaja turned and directed his attention upon it, the cloud increased in size and lightning began to flash. There he said, 'Now the thunder will start.' The words were hardly out of his mouth when the thunder began to roll loudly. In great delight, the Khwaja descended from his throne. Taking two or three steps, he stood facing the cloud. As he watched the flashes of the lightning and listened to the roar of the thunder, he laughed in his joy and delight. Then, just when the flashes of lightning were darting down, he repeated the invocation *Allahu Akbar* several times in a voice loud enough to be heard by all those who were there. He then returned to his throne, sat down, and said, 'Now the wind will blow from the direction of the cloud.' Immediately the wind, which had previously been coming from the south, did start to blow from that quarter. Then the clouds rose high in the sky with a great flurry and scurry, while the thunder rolled and the brilliant lightning dazzled the eyes of those who were watching. But then, relaxing the attention which he had been directing towards the clouds, the Khwaja said, 'This is not rain, but has turned into a chilly wind.' Having said this, he went to his house and all his disciples also went off to their own homes and lodgings. At that moment a chilly breeze sprang up, then stopped. There was no more thunder or lightning, and the clouds broke up and disappeared. Glory be to God for the sight of this wonderful spectacle, so mysteriously produced!

> The holy Khwaja wished for clouds:
> The thunder roared and lightning flashed.
> His whole desire thus came to pass,
> Before it vanished by his will.
> The clouds broke up, the storm did cease,
> The chill wind blew, then all was peace.

It should be known that it is impossible to describe properly in speech for writing the extent of the love which the Khwaja had for clouds, rain, lightning and the sound of thunder, or of his knowledge of the various types of clouds. It is true, though, that a part of this love and knowledge has been wonderfully revealed in some of his *Kafis*.

LESSON 20: THE KHWAJA'S DEVOTIONS—A BAN ON THE LOCAL MUSICIANS—AGAINST SHIA TENDENCIES—GREAT COOKS
THURSDAY, 1ST MUHARRAM, A.H. 1312 (4.7.94)

I was granted the supreme blessing of humble attendance upon the holy Khwaja in the evening.

The Khwaja was seated upon his throne, with a rosary in his hand, and was occupied with the exercise of repeating the words 'God, God' in a sufficiently loud voice for those present in the company to hear. From time to time he also spoke to those who were there, before once more resuming his devotional exercises, until the call to prayer was given, when he arose and performed the prayer. When he had finished praying he returned to his private devotions. He recited the Sura of the Tidings (Quran, 78), the verse of the Throne (Quran 2, 255), the Fateha (Quran, 1) and the Sura of the Unbelievers (Quran, 109)—all accompanied by the invocation of the name of God—also the verse 'The Apostle believed' (Quran, 2.284), down to the end, and this prayer: 'O Living and Eternal God, there is no God but You.' Besides these, he uttered many other prayers seeking for forgiveness and glorifying God, and other Suras of the Holy Quran. Finally he raised his hands, asking for God's blessing, and everyone went home, leaving the holy saint still occupied in his worship of God.

I have, however, recorded here what took place on this occasion. First a Hindu came. Rubbing his forehead on the ground, he then said, with hands folded in respect 'One of our people is having a wedding. If you will grant us your permission, we will summon the musicians of the town, in order that they may play the drums and tabors, and others musical instruments, which are essential parts of a wedding.' The Khwaja replied, 'The prohibition in force is one which I have laid exclusively on my own staff, not upon other townsfolk.' (It should be explained that the reason the Khwaja had ordered his staff not to invite the musicians of the town, and to keep them away from their weddings and other joyful occasions was that the musicians had begun to drink *bhang* and had also deviated somewhat from orthodox Sunni beliefs, as when they sometimes uttered discourtesies about the noble Companions of the Holy Prophet.[S.A.W.])

Then the Khwaja said, 'In the happy times of our Shaikh, Hazrat Sahib-ur-Rauza, there was a very learned religious scholar called Maulavi Ghulam Daud, who used to teach in Mithankot. He was a disciple of the saint, and a proper Sunni; but he felt a slightly greater love for Hazrat Ali than for the other noble Caliphs. This provoked his colleagues to seize hold of him, and bring him before our Shaikh. The saint asked. "O Ghulam Daud, what do you say about the companions of God's Apostle?" "Lord," he replied "All the Companions are true, but I have a greater love for Hazrat Ali because he is the Alpha and the Omega of all the Shaikhs and Pirs of the Way." Then the saint dismissed him. But for the rest of his life, no one would follow that Maulavi in prayer. How firm and strict to their orthodoxy the people of former times used to be! Although he was no heretic, the Maulavi was still derided and avoided by every one. Nowadays, though, there are thousands of people who talk a lot of foolish nonsense about the noble Companions yet still dare to call themselves orthodox believers!'

He continued, 'My own great Shaikh, Khwaja Fakhr-e-Jahan, used to say of anyone who loved Hazrat Ali more than the others Companions because he was the pir of his pirs, or because he was his ancestor—and it is obvious that everyone has a particular affection for his own forebears—or because that person had adopted the profession of valour, and loved Hazrat Ali for his courageousness, that all these kinds of love were the idle products of heresy, strictly to be avoided.'

Then he spoke of Marwar, saying, 'Believers are far outnumbered by unbelievers there. But such Muslims as do exist, even though they may be shaved like yogis or outcasts, are quite free from such forbidden practices as *bhang*-taking, and so on, and are very strict in their observance of the commandments of the Law. They are also regular in their consultation of orthodox religious authorities, whose instructions they faithfully follow.'

Later, there was a discussion of the relative skills of the holy kitchen, of how one cooked well, and another did not, and of how Miyan Ahmad Yar's art had surpassed that of all other cooks. The Khwaja said, 'Such was Ahmad Yar's ability and skill in the various branches of the culinary art that he was without peer in his own time. No one like him has yet entered our kitchens. Nawab Sadiq Muhammad Abbasi used to say,' he added, 'that he had two aims in going to Mithankot Sharif—one was to attend upon his pir, the other to eat Ahmad Yar's pilau!'

He then continued, 'Since the sons of Hazrat Qibla-e-Alam Maharawi were linked by ties of spiritual allegiance and devotion to our own saintly forebears, they frequently used to visit them. In honour of the fact that they were the pir's sons, several delicious dishes would be prepared for them, whenever any of them came Khwaja Nur Hasan, one of Hazrat Qibla-e-Alam's sons, once came here in the time of Khwaja Mahbub-e-Ilahi. Our Khwaja told his cooks to prepare all kinds of dishes each day and to take them to the house where Khwaja Nur Hasan was staying, since he was a special guest. They carried out his orders. But one day it happened to be raining heavily. Meat and other ingredients were unobtainable. The head of the kitchen, Khair Muhammad, came before the Shaikh and humbly expressed his apologies, saying, "Lord, because it is raining today, we cannot even get meat. Nor are the other delicacies getting cooked, for there is no firewood. So what can be prepared for the pir's son?" "Dry bread and lentils," said the saint. So this was what was prepared and brought before the pir's son. Now, although the food was both less and worse than usual, Khwaja Nur Hasan still asked, "What have you cooked today, Khair Muhammad?" He was overcome by trembling, afraid that he would be struck for not having prepared his usual delicious dishes. But, having no choice in the matter, he went up to him. Then the Khwaja took off a gold-embroidered cloth he was wearing and laid it round Khair Muhammad's shoulders, saying, "Up till now Hazrat Mahbub-e-Ilahi has been sending me food fit for his pir's son, but today he has sent me food fit for his slave. God be praised!'"

LESSON 21: THE KHWAJA'S DEVOTIONS—KHWAJA MUHAMMAD AQIL AND THE COURTESAN
SUNDAY, 4TH MUHARRAM, A.H. 1312 (7.7.94)

I was granted the supreme blessing of humble attendance upon the holy Khwaja in the evening.

The Khwaja was seated upon his throne, with a rosary in his hand. He was occupied in an exercise of denial and affirmation, dwelling first on the words, 'There is no God', then on 'but God', and finally on 'God'. Then he recited other verses and prayers, until at last he asked God's blessing, arose, and entered his house.

He did, however, say one thing during his devotions, which I have recorded. The unusual behaviour of the saints was being discussed, and people in the group were talking about the miracles of the greatest saints. Then the Khwaja said, 'One day a courtesan came with her musicians, hoping for a reward from our Qibla, Hazrat Sahib-ur-Rauza. Humbly she made her offering to him, then asked him for something. Our holy Shaikh told one of his servants, called Masud, to give her six glass beads. Respectfully putting her hands together, the courtesan said, "Lord I am indeed delighted with this gift, but would you please bestow it with your own holy hand?" so he took the beads back from Masud, and gave them to the woman with his own blessed hand. And from that day on the courtesan used to get a daily gratuity of six pieces of silver.'

LESSON 22: THE KHWAJA'S ABLUTIONS— BELIEF IN THE SAINTS—A MUSICAL PARTY
FRIDAY, 16TH MUHARRAM, A.H. 1322 (20.7.94)

I was granted the supreme blessing of humble attendance upon the holy Khwaja towards the end of the morning.

A letter arrived from Nawab Sadiq Muhammad Khan Abbasi, the fervent disciple of the holy Khwaja, invoking his blessing and seeking his healing powers for an illness which had afflicted him. He opened the envelope with his own blessed hand, read its contents, then wrote an answer with his holy pen.

Then he told someone to go and find out if the congregation was ready for the Friday prayer. A servant went, and came back to report that the congregation was ready. The Khwaja then arose, and performed his ablutions in the following fashion. First he washed both hands up to the wrists three times, then his blessed face from the hair-line on his forehead to the tip of his chin, also the patches behind his ears four times with great care. Then he washed his holy beard six times, that is to say, he poured water over all of it three times on each side, from the ear-lobes to the point of his chin, while rubbing it with his hand. Then he poured water once over the whole of his face. Then, with his fingers apart, he carefully wiped one lot of water over his entire head, both his ears, and his neck. Then he took the jug from the servant and washed both feet with his own hand, rubbing the cracks between his toes with the little finger of his left hand.

From the commencement of his ablutions as far as the wiping of his head, the Khwaja got his servant to pour the water, but when he washed his feet, he took the jug to complete his ablutions himself. Roughly twelve *sers* of water must have been used in his ablutions; for there were three jugs, two large ones holding about five *sers* each, and a small one containing two *sers*.

Anyway, after the Khwaja's ablutions were completed, this humble servant, who had the whole time been observing the manner of their performance, with the intention of recording it, went to the place of washing before the prayer. I thought to myself—and this was most disrespectful of me—that perhaps a hair might have fallen from the Khwaja's holy beard or blessed head. So I searched until I found a single thread of hair from his holy beard. Picking up this precious relic, I kept it for use as an amulet.

The Khwaja then went to the large mosque and conducted the Friday prayer. After this was over, the topic of belief in the holy saints was raised, and the Khwaja said, 'Shaikh Junaid once told a disciple not to go near Yusuf Husain Razi, the reason being that he was afraid he might go, and not believe in him when he had seen him; for Yusuf Husain Razi was an outwardly unorthodox Malamati, whom some believed in, but others denied. Since that disciple was a proper Sufi, he did go to see him. When he returned, the Shaikh asked him, "Did you go to Yusuf, my son?" "Yes, I did," he replied. "Have you come back believing in him, or not?" the Shaikh asked. "Believing in him," he said. "Praise be to God," said the Shaikh, "if you had not come back believing in him, your faith would have suffered."'

The Khwaja then commented, 'When faith suffers by refusing to believe in the holy company of saints, what can be the state of the faith of those who vilify and insult them?' (The Khwaja then said that pride was of four kinds, and explained each type. But since those types have already been described in detail in Lesson 18, I have not repeated them here.)

The Khwaja then asked for mangoes to be brought. A basket of delicious mangoes was produced. He signed to the servants to set this in front of him. His noble son, Khwaja Muhammad Bakhsh, was there, and the Khwaja told him, 'Give five mangoes to Rukn ud-Din!' So his son graciously bestowed five mangoes on this poor creature. The rest of the mangoes were shared out among the others in the company.

Then the Khwaja told his musician, Barkat Ali, a master of music and singing, to bring his harmonium and play. So he went home to get his harmonium. When he returned the Khwaja's presence, he played it and sang some poems. Through the spiritual grace of the company of the holy Khwaja, all those who were there had the most delightful time. What a happy occasion that was!

Lesson 23: Lessons 9-14 Produced
Saturday, 17th Muharram, A.H. 1312 (21.7.94)

I was granted the supreme blessing of humble attendance upon the holy Khwaja in the afternoon.

I had under my arm several pages which I had put together, containing Lessons 9-14. He asked me to give him these, so I reverently handed them to him. After casting his eyes over them, he smiled and said, 'I have had a look at these today. Another day you must read them out and I shall listen.'

Lesson 24: On Unlucky Days—On Regard for One's Mother—
The Khwaja Swallows Verses of Healing
Friday, 24th Muharram, A.H. 1312 (27.7.94)

I was granted the supreme blessing of humble attendance upon the holy Khwaja in the afternoon.

The talk turned to the subject of leaving home on a Wednesday, and the Khwaja said, 'It is forbidden to take leave of one's Shaikh or to go out of one's house on a Wednesday for the purposes of travel. But it is not forbidden for a person who is travelling to arrive home on a Wednesday.' At this point one of those present asked if it was true that intercourse with one's lawfully wedded wife on that day had also been forbidden. The Khwaja said there was no such prohibition.

Then I asked, 'Lord, what of the popular belief—held especially by women—that it is not permitted to bathe, to massage oneself with oil, to wear new clothes on a Saturday or a Tuesday?'

The Khwaja replied by telling how he had one day been seated before his Shaikh, Khwaja Fakhr-e-Jahan, when he told a servant to bring oil and massage his head. 'But, Lord,' said the servant, 'today is Tuesday.' The saint upheld his objection, and did not have an oil massage that day. But when on another occasion the Shaikh asked for oil to be brought and someone said, 'Today is Tuesday,' he overruled his objection by saying 'So what?' and so the servant did bring oil, and massaged his head.

The Khwaja concluded by saying that, so far as the three activities mentioned on these days were concerned, the best course of action was a mixture of observance and disregard—in other words, sometimes to perform them, sometimes not.

Then one of the chief disciples prostrated himself and said, 'There is a poor woman who humbly represents that her son, a government official, is far away from her. She is ill with the distress caused by this separation from her son, and wants him to be transferred from that distant post to somewhere near here.'

'Write from me,' the Khwaja replied, 'to the officer who is her son's superior, so that he may transfer him.'

'There was once a Shaikh in Shiraz,' he continued, 'who used to ask everyone who went to him and said he was going on the Pilgrimage, whether his mother was alive or dead. If he said she was alive, he would stop him going and tell him that his Pilgrimage was to look after his mother, so to go back and be with her.'

Then someone brought out from under his arm a china dish on which were written verses of healing from the Holy Quran. Reverently he handed this dish to the Khwaja, who took it in his two blessed hands, moved his true-speaking tongue over what had been written, and swallowed it. It should be explained that in those days an illness had attacked the holy body of the Khwaja, and someone had been appointed to write verses of healing in saffron on a china dish, which he used to present daily.

CONCLUSION

This is the end of the first part of The Lessons of the Meetings, which contains the fruits of three years' teachings. The future utterances of the holy Khwaja will be recorded in a second part, if God so wills.

It should be realized that everything in this entire book consists only of what I have heard with my own ears or seen with my own eyes, at first hand. Many of my fellow-disciples have often told me that they had heard the Khwaja say such and such a thing, which I ought to write down, since they could remember it perfectly; but while not doubting their reliability, I have never agreed to such suggestions.

I hope that the book will interest its readers, and that they will remember its poor writer in their prayers. I trust too that they will disregard my humble part in its production, and see past me to its real author, the holy Khwaja, who has read and listened to it all from beginning to end, and has corrected its errors in his own hand.

> There stands no real bar between us, love,
> No, nothing but an idle thought...

The Poems

of Khwaja Ghulam Farid

Part I

Poems of Faith and Instruction

The first four poems deal in different ways with the rejection of the world. In '*Lord have mercy*' the poet confesses his sins and makes a humble plea for divine forgiveness, while in '*We'll set out*' he hopes for deliverance. '*So what?*' is pointed questioning of the worth of worldly prestige, and the transience of false objects of devotion is exposed in '*Where are those lovers now?*'.

After this prelude, the central group of poems deal directly with the mystical teachings of Sufism, whose core is neatly summarised by the twin titles of '*Learn yourself to recognize*' and '*He is present everywhere.*' These lead naturally to the revelation of '*You are the All*', which is expressed most beautifully with a more complex use of theological language in '*The heart*'. The following poems turn to the expression of the experience of mystical love. Our hidden secret begins with a direct outpouring of distress, before going on to contrast the blindness of more outward religious observance with the true insight of the great Sufis, however unorthodox they might superficially appear. '*Now passion is my lot*' is a simple expression of what such insight entails, which is developed most ingeniously in the long and splendid address to an imagined mullah, '*All I know is A*'. The consequences of mystical passion are clearly set forth in '*The true delights of ecstasy*'.

The final set of poems are connected by being addressed to different objects of the poet's devotion. The Sindhi poem '*To this love be fair*', is a direct invocation to the divine Beloved. In one of the simpler poems connected with Khwaja Farid's performance of the Pilgrimage, '*On approaching Medina*', he expresses his profound attachment to the Prophet. The short '*Take him as your guide*' combines monistic teaching with a statement of love for his elder brother and pir, Khwaja Fakhr ud Din. '*To Khwaja Nur Muhammad*' is a eulogy of the ancestral pir of Khwaja Farid's family. Lastly, the '*Ode to Sadiq Khan*', addressed to his temporal ruler and spiritual disciple, the Nawab of Bahawalpur, is conventional in tone, but interesting as the only direct expression of political views in Khwaja Farid's poetry.

1 Lord Have Mercy

From wicked lust and thieving fraud
Preserve me in Your mercy, Lord.

All evil ways and evil deeds
Have I a thousand times abjured.

As I repent my many sins,
With Your forgiveness me reward.

The saints and prophets are Your slaves:
You are our mighty Overlord.

At last when friend and foe are one
May I be of Your grace assured.

How ugly, foul, and full of faults
Am I, by all to be abhorred.

Your glory is Your perfect grace,
While I by countless faults am flawed.

How bitterly I weep and moan
When I my long-done sins record.

On Doomsday, rising from the grave,
Those sins will sound in disaccord.

Through You alone can poor Farid
Salvation's vessel hope to board.

1

چوریوں چاریوں استغفار
بخشم شالا رب غفار

گندڑی عادت گندڑے فعلوں
توبہ توبہ لکھ لکھ وار

کر کر سخت گناہ پرتا پیم
توں ہیں خاوند بخشن ہار

پیر پیغمبر تیڈے بانہیں
توں مالک توں کل مختار

میں بد عملی تے کر رحمت
جیں ڈینھ یار وی یار نہ یار

اوگن ہاری نہ کہیں کم دی
کوجھی کملی بد کردار

تیڈا شان ہے فضل کرم دا
میں وچ ڈوہ تے عیب ہزار

آون یاد گناہ پرانے
پٹ پٹ رووں زارو زار

رات قبر دی ڈینھ حشر دا
سر تے کڑ کم بارے بار

میں مسکین فرید ہاں تیڈا
توں بن کون اتارم پار

2 We'll Set Out

These dwellings shall deserted lie:
We'll set out early or late.

Two days among these folk we'll stay,
Before like geese we migrate.

How strange we find this foreign land,
This falsely founded estate.

I have no comrade, so to whom
Should I my sorrows relate?

Would any choose to visit earth?
I came here only through fate.

I'm on my way to that fair realm—
May God deliver me straight!

Unite me with my love, O Lord!
To you this prayer I state.

Much grief has love bestowed on me,
And struck with sufferings great.

2

صبا ھیں سنجھ صبا ھیں
خالی رہسن جائیں

پکھی پردیسی ابھے سردے
دو دن دے خلقائیں

ملک بیگانہ دیس پرایا
کوجھیاں کوڑ بنائیں

نہ کوئی ساتھی نہ کوئی سنگتی
کینوں درد سنائیں

قسمت سانگے ڈٹھم اے دھرتی
آندا کون اٹھائیں

حسن نگر ڈوں تھیوم روانہ
یا ربّ توڑ پچائیں

منگاں دعائیں لله سائیں
وچھڑیا ڈھول ملائیں

عشق فرید بہوں ڈکھ ڈتڑے
بچھیاں برہوں بلائیں

3 So What?

You may hold the world in fee—
So what though, even then?
Disappearance is the key!

Muslims all may bow to your
Spiritual authority—
So what though, even than?

Study of the scriptures may
Grant you learning's mastery—
So what though, even then?

All the world you may command,
Robed in royal dignity—
So what though, even then?

Fame you may have gained to go
Off to heaven merrily—
So what though, even then?

Sunni pure and Hanfi,
Sufi also you may be—
So what though, even then?

Or in outward shape and form
Your beloved you may see—
So what though, even then?

'Shaikh of Shaikhs' you may be called,
Ranked most high in sanctity—
So what though, even then?

India's every quarter may
Honour you for poetry—
So what though, even then?

3

تھئ تابع خلاقت سب
تاں وی کیا تھی پیا
ھئ گم تھیون مطلب

تیڈا رشد ارشاد وی تونے
وچ پہنتا عجم عرب
تاں وی کیا تھی پیا

پڑھ پڑھ بید پران صحائف
پیا سکھیوں علم ادب
تاں وی کیا تھی پیا

سارے جگ تے حکم چلاویں
پا شاہی دا منصب
تاں وی کیا تھی پیا

دنیاں دے وچ عزت پایو
گیوں عقبیٰ نال طرب
تاں وی کیا تھی پیا

سنی پاک تے حنفی مذہب
رکھیو صوفی دا مشرب
تاں وی کیا تھی پیا

وچ آثار افعال صفاتیں
جے یار گھدوئی لبھ
تاں وی کیا تھی پیا

غوثی قطبی رتبہ پا تو
تھیوں شیخ شیوخ لقب
تاں وی کیا تھی پیا

شعر فرید تیڈا وچ ٹلیا
ہند ماڑ دکھن پورب
تاں وی کیا تھی پیا

4 Where Are Those Lovers Now?

Love God alone: let not your heart
To other idle fancies veer.

Where now do Laila and Majnun
Or Sohni and her herd appear?

Where now is Ranjha, where the Kheras,
Where are those Sials and Hir?

Where now are Sassi and Punnun
And where their sufferings severe?

Where now are Saifal and the fairies,
Where their times of grief and cheer?

Except the One Reality
All things will surely disappear.

The goatherds gladly leap about
But spring comes briefly in the year.

For everything save God alone
Is false and vain—of this be clear.

Farid, my love forgets me not:
No room is there for doubting here.

4

سٹ سک غیر خدا دی
سب شے وہم خیال

کتھ لیلیٰ کتھ مجنوں
کتھ سوہنی میینوال

کتھ رانجھن کتھ کھیڑے
کتھ ہے ہیر سیال

کتھ سسی کتھ پنوں
کتھ او درد کشال

کتھ سیغل کتھ پریاں
کتھ او ہجر وصال

باجھوں عہد حقیقی
کل شے عین زوال

چار ڈیہاڑے چیتر دے
کڈھے کبروال

ما خلا اللہ باطل
بیٹھک کوڑ پیال

یار فرید نہ وسرم
مشکل محض محال

5 Learn Yourself To Recognise

Where is the land from which you came?
From what domain did you arise, oh?
Why do you wander sick at heart,
Whose dwelling in love's city lies, oh?

Why flee or seek the world's delights?
Why turn from life like one in pain?
Why, rubbing ashes on your limbs,
Should you maintain a yogi's guise, oh?

Now of yourself take careful stock
And see things as they truly are—
And whether He will come or not
Fret not yourself with vain surmise, oh!

You are identical with Him,
Not just alike or similar:
In essence and in attributes
Now learn yourself to recognise, oh!

Think deeply on these words of mine
And hearken in your inmost heart—
Of both the worlds you are the lord,
Whose succour God alone supplies, oh!

5

کس دھرتی سے آئے ہو تم
کس نگری کے باسی رے
پرم نگر ہے دیس تمھارا
پھرتے کہاں اداسی رے

کیوں ہوتے ہو جوگی بھوگی
روگی طرح براگی رے
انگ بھبھوت رما کے کیوں کر
رکھتے بدن سنیاسی رے

اپنا آپ سنبھال کے دیکھو
کرکے نظر حقیقت کی
فکر نہ کیجیو یارو ہر گز
آسی یا نہ آسی رے

تم ہو ساگی تم ہو ساگی
واگی ذرا نہ واگی رے
اپنی ذات صفات کو سمجھو
اپنی کرو شناسی رے

بات فرید سوچ کے سنیو
لاکر دل کے کانوں کو
دونوں جگ کے مالک تم ہو
بھولے اللہ راسی رے

6 He Is Present Everywhere

See, Punnal's present everywhere—
All mystics mark and hear!

'There is no thing resembling Him'[1]
Know only He is here.

'The visage of your Lord endures'[2]
All else shall disappear.

'To want for nothing, only God'
Confirms the true fakir.

That 'nought exists save God alone'
Our faith is sure and clear.

That all but God is vain and false
Should be your one idea.

Mere knowledge, lacking mystic art,
Can only interfere.

---

[1]   Quran 42:11
[2]   Quran 55:27

6

هر جا ذات پنل ہے
صوفی سمجھ سنجان

لَیْسَ کَمِثْلِہٖ شَیْئٌ
سب شے اس نوں جان

یَبْقٰی وَجْہُ رَبِّکَ
باقی کل شے فان

لَا یُحْتَاجُ سِوَی اللہ
ہے فقر دا شان

لَا مَوْجُوْدَ سِوَی اللہ
ساڈا دین ایمان

حق باجھوں بیو باطل
دھیان رکھیں ہر آن

علم فرید ہے حاجب
بے شک بے عرفان

7 You Are The All

You are the All, the Whole, whom none
As single or a part should view.

You are the lord of paradise,
You are the rose and bulbul too.

The earth is yours and so is heaven:
Who of your worth has any clue?

Because Mansur has been impaled,
His brethren make a strange to-do.

You're Spirit, Likeness, Witnessing[1]—
To this reality be true!

In heaven, limbo, and on earth
There's no one who can equal you.

Your love, Farid, dwells at your side—
So why this idle search pursue?

---

[1]   Ascending worlds of spiritual reality.

7

کیویں توں فرد تے جزو سڈاویں
توں کلی توں کل

باغ بہشت دا توں ہیں مالک
خود بلبل خود گل

عرش وی تیڈا فرش وی تیڈا
توں عالی انمل

چڑھ داریں منصور دے بھائی
کرن عجب غلغل

روح مثال شہادت توں ہیں
سمجھ سنجان نہ بھل

دنیا عقبیٰ برزخ اندر
نا ہیں تیڈڑا تل

یار فریدا کول ہے تیڈے
نہ بیہودہ رل

8 The Heart

The world is but an idle dream,
Its shapes a film upon a stream.

If you would know reality,
Then listen carefully, mark and see
That oneness is a mighty sea,
Where pluralism's bubbles teem.

Duality of base is bare,
Which pride alone as child can bear:
It vanishes when picked of air,
And all again does water seem.

Put not your trust in the *Kifaya*:
Be guided not by the *Hidaya*,
And tear to pieces you *Wiqaya*[1]—
This heart as your Quran esteem.

The heart knows passion's gnostic art
And all that sacred books impart:
All being's life lies in the heart,
The door to mysteries supreme.

The heart contains creation's soul:
It is the world's one final goal,
Placed at the centre of the whole—
All else is but a cloud of steam.

Behind this clear Humanity
Is placed ideal Sovereignty,
Then Power and Divinity[2]—
The heart holds being's every scheme.

---

[1]   The titles of standard legal texts.

[2]   The four ascending worlds of the spirit.

8

جگ وہم خیال تے خواب ے
سب صورت نقش بر آب ے

جے پچھیں حال حقیقت
سن سمجھ اتے رکھ عبرت
جیویں بحر محیط ہے وحدت
کل کثرت شکل حباب ے

نہیں اصلوں اصل دوئی دا
خود جان ہے نسل دوئی دا
گیا پھوکا نکل دوئی دا
ول اوہی آب دا آب ے

نا کافی جان کفایہ
نا ہادی سمجھ ہدایہ
کر پرزے جلد وقایہ
ایہا دل قرآن کتاب ے

ہے پرم گیان وی دلڑی
ہے بید پران وی دلڑی
ہے جان جہان وی دلڑی
دل بطن بطون دا باب ے

دل لب ہے کون مکاں دا
دل غایت اصل جہاں دا
دل مرکز زمین زماں دا
بیا کوڑ پلال حجاب ے

وچ صورت دے ناسوتی
وچ معنے دے ملکوتی
جبروت اتے لاہوتی
دل اندر سب اسباب ے

Try of yourself to be aware,
Of mere discipleship beware:
For distance from the heart have care,
Which causes suffering extreme.

رکھ انتر دھیان فریدی

سٹ سکھڑیں پیر مریدی

ہے دوری سخت بعیدی

جی سکھڑیں کان عذابے

9 Our Hidden Secret

My darling finds me quite displeasing:
So what should I wear nose-rings for?

I care not for my parting's neatness,
For rouge's blush or kohl's completeness:
Far off dwells he whom I adore.

In this my ancient passion's madness
I ever brood in deepest sadness:
My love is stitched in every pore.

Our wealth lies in his airy graces:
We bow towards his dusty paces
Which are eternal beauty's spoor.

My girl-friends on their couches' covers
With bangled arms embrace their lovers:
Just I am trapped in sorrow sore.

These desert paths are Aiman's valley
Along which his dear camels sally,
These gravel dunes the mount of Tur.

We bear the mullah's castigation,
Unable from their wretched station
Our hidden secret to explore.

How we detest the mullah's preaching!
In holy Ibn ul Arabi's teaching
Our faith stands confident and sure.

We lovers in our rapture balmy
Cry 'Mine is glory' like Bistami,
Or 'I am Truth' as did Mansur.

9

بولا یینسر کس نوں پاواں
ڈھولن کیتم نا منظور

کتھ نوں بیناں مانگھ بناواں
کجلا پاواں سرخی لاواں
یار تتی دا وسدا دور

پیت پرانی کملا کیتا
عشق اولڑا لوں لوں سیتا
پون کللڑے پل پل پور

طرز نیاز ساڈی موڑی
قبلہ قد میں یار دی دھوڑی
حسن ازل دی چال غرور

سینگیاں سرتیاں سمجھ وچھاون
بانہہ چڑیلی ور گل لاون
ہک میں مفت رہی مجبور

وادی ایمن تھل دے چارے
جتھاں برو چل کر ہوں قطارے
نکڑے مٹڑے ہن کوہ طور

ملاں مارن سخت ستاون
گجھڑے راز دا بھیت نہ پاون
بے وس شودے ہن معذور

ملوانے دے وعظ نہ بھانے
بے شک ساڈا دین ایمانے
ابن العربی دی دستور

عاشق مست مدام ملامی
کہہ سبحانی بن بسطامی
آکھ انا الحق تھی منصور

In beauty-worship lies devotion
And blessedness in passion's potion—
In absence presence find therefore.

And so my way is quite inverted—
All prayers and fasts have I deserted:
My waywardness is not obscure!

حسن پرستی عین عبادت
شاہد مستی صرف سعادت
غیبت غفلت محض حضور

ریت فرید دی پھٹڑی ساری
رہندا صوم صلواتوں عاری
رندی مشرب ہے مشہور

10 Now Passion Is My Lot

Now passion is my lot
Of other tasks I'm shot.

When once I tasted love's delights
All sorrows I forgot.

Of love these withered mullahs can
Not understand a jot.

The teaching of my Lord undid
The Law's entangled knot.

When taught the lesson 'All is He'
Enlightment I got.

Although my head be shattered, yet
Aside will I turn not.

I have no other wants, Farid,
For love my hunger's hot.

10

برہوں پیو سے پکھڑے
بے کل دھندھڑے چکڑے

پیت پرم دی چاشنی چکھڑیم
وسرے ڈکھڑے پکھڑے

عشق دی بات نہ سمجھن اصلوں
اے ملوانے رکھڑے

اَڈّ بَنی رَبّی جب ہویا
شرع مسائل سکڑے

ہمہ اوست دا سبق گھدوسے
فاش تھئے کجھ لکڑے

ہیں بلاہوں نا پھرساں تونے
سر گھیسم سو ٹکڑے

محض فرید نہیں کئی حاجت
ہیوں ہک نینھ دے بکھڑے

11 All I Know Is A

All I know is A, sir!

No other story pleases me:
My heart is won by A, sir.

Of B and C I nothing know,
Made powerless by A, sir.

Now put those books of law aside:
Just teach me love, I pray, sir.

You'd tell your children if you had
To love once fallen prey, sir.

Unless you give a class in love
I'll leave your school today, sir.

If love you learn and love you teach,
Hurray for you, huray for you , sir

Forgetting other lusts, in life
And death my love's I'll stay, sir.

Oh blow the spell of love on me
And break this languor's sway, sir.

To husband, wealth or home's delights
No further care I pay, sir.

Oh Ranjha's mine and I am his:
What can those Kheras say, sir?

My home I'll leave to settle where
The sky with clouds is grey, sir.

11

الف بكو ہم بس وے میاں جی

ہور کہانی مول نہ بھانی
الف گیوم دل کھس وے میاں جی

بے تے دی ہئی کل نہ کائی
الف کیتم بے وس وے میاں جی

ٹھپّ رکھ فقہ اصول دے مسئلے
باب برہوں دا ڈس وے میاں جی

جے کر لگڑو چاٹ برہوں دی
جایاں کوں ڈیسیں ڈس وے میاں جی

جے نہ سبق برہوں دا ڈتڑو
اج کلھ ویساں نس وے میاں جی

برہوں سکھیں تے برہوں سکھائیں
ہئی شاباس شاباس وے میاں جی

جیندیں موئیں ہک یار دے رہسوں
وسری ہور ہوس وے میاں جی

منتر پریت دا چھوک شکاریں
لنگڑیں ہم آلس وے میاں جی

الفت زر دی گھر دی ور دی
نا رہ گئی ہک خس وے میاں جی

رانجھن میڈا میں رانجھن دی
کھیڑیاں دے منہ بھس وے میاں جی

سٹ گھر بار تے بار وسیساں
بدلیں کیتی لس وے میاں جی

Through love, once understood, you'll put
Your righteousness away, sir.

For love at last I'll give my life:
Suppose not that I play, sir.

My love was written when there was
Of pen and ink no trace, sir.

I have not turned to him just now:
I have been his for ay, sir.

I'll not leave love, which gives to me
Renewed delight each day, sir!

علم عمل بھل ویسی جیکر
عشق پیو کن رس وے میاں جی

اوڑک عشق اندر جند ڈیسوں
نہ سمجھیں کھل ہس وے میاں جی

نیݨھ کڈ وکڑاں پیوسے پکھڑے
نہ ہئی قلم تے مس وے میاں جی

نہ اج کلھ دی یار دے ول دی
روز ازل دی ہس وے میاں جی

عشقوں مول فرید نہ پھرساں
روز نویں ہم چس وے میاں جی

12 The True Delights Of Ecstasy

Have any felt besides fakirs
The true delights of ecstasy?

The All in all things have I seen
And learnt what 'All is He' does mean,
And with the holy help of pirs
Have drunk the wine of unity.

When drunkenness displays its grace
For bareness only in there place:
My habit shredded now appears,
Instead I wear immodesty.

How blessed is those sufferers' pain,
Their load of love and sore disdain!
Yes, to their sorrows smouldering fierce
I offer all prosperity.

How many homes has beauty wrecked!
See—through the jungle-paths have trekked
A hundred Sassis, lakhs of Hirs:
For such is passion's savagery.

12

کیں پایا باجھ فقیراں
جذبۂ عشق کی لذت کو

کل شے وچ کل شے ڈیٹھوسے
ہمہ اوست دا درس کیتوسے
برکت صحبت پیراں
پی کر بادۂ وحدت کو

جب مدہوشی ناز ڈکھایا
عریانی نے رنگ جمایا
خرقہ پاڑ لویراں
پہنیم رندی خلعت کو

درد منداں کوں درد سلامت
بار محبت پنڈ ملامت
دکھ دکھ اٹھدیاں پیڑاں
گھول گھتاں سب راحت کو

حسن فرید کئی گھر لوٹے
رلدیاں پھردیاں جنگل بوٹے
سے سیساں لکھ حیراں
ڈیکھو عشق دی شدت کو

13 To This Love Be Fair

Come, to this love of mine be fair:
For all my pain, your thanks I'll sing.

To you I'll bow, to you repair,
And at your feet my head I'll fling.

How should I praise your beauty rare?
My life in sacrifice I'll bring.

This solemnly to you I'll swear—
Of all my being you are king.

You fill my thoughts, I do declare,
For you I find in every thing.

Though of your love I may despair
Yet still to you I'll humbly cling.

13

عشق اسانجھی جا آہے انصاف
ظلم نبھائیندس تاں بھی تہنجا تھورا گائیندس

سجدہ جانب تہنجی تہنجے گرد طواف
قدم قدم تے سمیس نوائیندس

تہنجی سیرت صورت سوہنی کنویں کیاں اوصاف
جندڑی توں توں گھول گھمائیندس

تن من سوہنا ملک ہے تہنجا سچ آہے نا ہے لاف
قسم اوھان جے سر جی کھائیندس

ذکرایں فکر ہے تہنجا دم دم چوئیندس صاف جا صاف
عبد معبود میں توکھے پائیندس

باندی گھولی یار دی آہیاں نا ہے فرید خلاف
آہیں کھے بھائیندس خواہ نہ بھائیندس

14 On Approaching Medina

To this, Medina's view
Am I devoted quite.

Now sweetly can I sleep:
All ancient griefs take flight.

Weep not, unhappy heart,
Whom pain no more shall smite.

Eclipsed are sun and moon
By this resplendent sight.

His noble dwelling is
A mirror of the Light.

Amidst Arabia's land
It glitters, jewel-bright.

All those who bear true faith
Will gain their heart's delight.

Downcast is Satan now:
Destroyed is selfhood's blight.

By angels am I told,
'We'll meet on Thursday night!'

14

تھیواں صدقے صدقے
آیا شہر مدینہ

سکھ دی سیبجھ سہایم
گیا ڈکھڑا دیرینہ

نہ رو دلڑی لٹڑی
نہ ڈکھ سنجرا سینہ

سجھ سونے دا ابھریا
ڈٹھڑا نیک مہینہ

حرم معلا روشن
ہے نوری آئینہ

عرب دی ساری دھرتی
سوہنی صاف نگینہ

ملسی جیڑھا رکھسی
صدق ثبوت یقینہ

تھیا شیطان پسیلا
مر گیا نفس کمینہ

خبر فرید سنیو سے
ملسوں شب آدینہ

15 Take Him As Your Guide

Come take your darling as your guide
And cast all other loves aside.

Just see your love in every form—
All else by him is nullified.

By knowing numbers all are One
Plurality is falsified.

In yearning for sweet Fakhr ud-Din
My sighs with smoking fires have vied.

To be with him will be your fate
When once your self you have denied.

15

یار کوں کر مسجود
چھڈ ڈے بیو معبود

ہر صورت وچ یار کوں جانیں
غیر نہیں موجود

سبھ اعداد کوں سمجھیں واحد
کثرت ہے مفقود

فخرالدین منٹھل دے شوقوں
دم دم تکلم دود

وصل فرید کوں حاصل ہویا
جب ہو گیا نابود

16 To Khwaja Nur Muhammad

Khwaja Nur Muhammad, oh!
You are our heart's delight.

Our reputation's in your hands:
Preserve our honour bright.

Punjab and Sindh and all the world
Bow down before your might.

All lands with loudly ringing call
Your bounty's praise indite.

Since in your steps lies all my luck
In this my court alight.

Oh darling second Joseph, grant
Me of your face a sight.

Beloved bridegroom of Mahar,
Hold me, your lover, tight.

By coming to Farid, my dear,
These thirsting eyes excite.

16

ساڈا دوست دلیں دا نور محمد خواجہ
ڈھولا یار چھیندا نور محمد خواجہ

ساری ساڈی شرم بھرم دا
تیڈے گل وچ لا جا

عرب وی تیڈی عجم وی تیڈی
سندھ پنجاب دا راجا

زمین زمن وچ وچ وجدا گجدا
فیض تیڈے دا واجا

قدم تیڈے وچ نوں من بھاگم
انگن میرے پوں پا جا

دلبر جانی یوسف ثانی
موہن مکھ ڈکھلا جا

نوشہ شہر مہار دا بنڑا
سکدی کوں گل لا جا

نین فرید دے درس پیاسے
آجا ناں ترسا جا

17 Ode To Sadiq Khan

Sadiq Khan, installed in state,
This realm may you uphold!

Come occupy your jewelled throne,
Let royal dignity be shown:
No British overlordship own—
To rule yourself be bold.

All tremble when they hear your name,
Kings die in fear before your fame,
Navabs and Mirs themselves proclaim
Your slaves, unbought by gold.

The holy men support your cause,
And true remain your governors,
While, wise as Plato, counsellors
Are in your court enrolled.

Attracted by your bounty's call
Have come and gone rewarded all—
The young and strong, the children small,
Besides the weak and old.

Enjoy your youthful season well
And by my side forever dwell,
For by your peerless graces' spell
My heart is quite controlled.

Unceasingly Farid does pray
Beloved, may you live for ay:
For dear indeed, sweet lord, I say
Do we each other hold.

17

صبح صادق خاں صاحبی مانے
پا سہرے گانے گہنے

سہجوں پھلوں سمجھ سہا توں
بخت تے تخت کوں جوڑ چھکا توں
اپنے ملک نوں آپ وسا توں
پٹ انگریزی تھانے

سن اقبال تیڈا پے ڈردے
راجے دہشت کھا کر مردے
میر نواب تھئے آبردے
بے زر مفت وکانے

پیر فقیر تیکوں سب چھندے
صوبیدار ملازم رہندے
گردا گرد کچہری بہندے
افلاطون سیانے

فیض تیڈے دے جگ وچ قصے
زالاں مرد گئے گھن حصے
نینگر تکڑے بڈھڑے لسے
نندھڑے بال ایانے

خوب ہنڈائیں جند جوانی
ہر دم کول وسیں دل جانی
یار پیارا یوسف ثانی
ناز تیڈے من بھانے

کرے فرید ہمیش دعائیں
سانول جیویں چر جگ تائیں
تیڈے ساڈا سوہنا سائیں
لگڑے نینہہ پرانے

Part II

Lyrics of Love and Distress

The poems in this section all deal with the central theme of Khwaja Farid's poetry, the lyrical expression of distress. '*He does not care*' is a simple outpouring of despair. In '*These eyes so keen*' and '*love's cruel smart*' most effective use in made of the love-imagery of the *ghazal*. A simpler style of lament, closer to the folk-song, prevails in '*What painful love is this?*', '*Sorrow-struck I grieve*' (made especially poignant by the short meter), and '*I'm lost*'. The same style is developed in more elaborate fashion in '*Your love will I bear yet*' with its exceptionally long stanzas, and the long '*The omens parting prophesy*', with its extraordinary rhetorical elaboration of the imagery of distress. Sad appeals are made in more straightforward fashion in '*May he come*' and '*My heart is but a pawn*'. '*Rano end my pain*' introduces references to the legend of Mumal, while the next poems '*Leaving me distraught*', '*My thought to whom should I confide?*', and the Persian—Siraiki macaronic '*I seek the wilderness's air*' draw on the story of Sassi, which is so clearly the local romance which meant most to Khwaja Farid. The Sassi-imagery also colours '*How strange is passion's pain*', while it is intertwined with references to Sohni's crossing of the river Chenab in '*I'll bear this passion's ache*'. The poet's resolve not to abandon his love, however painful it prove, is then expressed through the personage of Hir in '*My thoughts on Ranjha's land are bent*', before speaking again through Sassi in the little '*Go now and be his*'.

18 He Does Not Care

My life is spent in tears
And yet he does not care.

I've thrown my ornaments away
Of me he's unaware.

So far he's gone and comes not back
I'll perish in this snare.

No love is this but raging fire
Which in my heart does flare.

My youthful beauty all is gone
Destroyed in my despair.

In longing for sweet Fakhr ud-Din
My grief grows greater e'er.

My darling does not come to me
This pain for nought I bear.

18

روندیں عمر نبھائی
یار دی خبر نہ کائی

بھاگ سہاگ سنگار ونجایم
دلوں وساریا ماہی

دور گیا ول آیا ناہیں
مرساں کھا کر بھائی

عشق نہیں ہے نار غضب دی
چنگ چوانتی لائی

جوبن سارا روپ گنوایم
دردیں مار مسائی

فخرالدین مٹھل دے عشقوں
دم دم پیڑ سوائی

یار فرید نہ پایم پھیرا
گل گیوم مفت اجائی

19 These Eyes So Keen

These eyes so keen to fight
With war are never done:
Their looks are deadly quite
As spear, or dart, or gun.

These snaking locks and scorpion brows
Inflict their cruel bite,
And make my heart's blood run.

His gentle form and stony heart
Seem scarce to fit aright—
But mercy has he none.

As royal robe despatched by love
I bear this visage white,
While inward griefs me stun.

Since love has stripped away my shame
And all my honour bright,
Endurance now I shun.

Tormented is my state, Farid—
I am through passion's blight
In death and life undone.

19

غمزے کر دے جنگ
لڑ دے مول نہ اڑ دے
نیزے تیر تفنگ
قہری ناز نظر دے

زلف ہے بشیر ابرو بچھوئے
مارن ڈنگ نسنگ
چکدے زخم جگر دے

سانول دی ہے طرز انوکھی
تن نازک دل سنگ
ذرہ مہر نہ کر دے

برہوں اسا نوں خلعت بھیجی
ساوا پیلا رنگ
سو سو سول اندر دے

عشق ونجایم شرم بھرم کوں
گیا ناموس تے ننگ
گزرے وقت صبر دے

حال فرید دا دکھ ڈہیلا
دلڑی کیتس ننگ
نا جیندے نا مر دے

20 Love's Cruel Smart

I sit and weep my life away:
Through love all joys are gone astray.

My dark one's lovely line of kohl
Attacks me like a sword.
His eyes despatch their deadly darts:
His lashes war assay.

His amorous looks and graceful airs,
His jesting words of love,
His beauty, fairness—all enchant
My heart in every way.

My tears pour down from reddened lids,
My lashes are quite gone.
These eyes that people think inflamed
Love's cruel smart betray.

Reproaches, jeers, and anxious care
Have fallen to my lot.
The troubles of this love of mine
My lonely heart dismay.

Disgraced for nought I sorely rue
The taunts of all the town.
My love does not come near Farid,
Of fate the foregone prey.

20

بیٹھی رو رو عمر نبھایاں
سبھے خوشیاں عشق ونجایاں

واہ سانول دی دھار کجل دی
بے شک تیغ اجل دی
دیداں تیر چلائن کاری
پلکاں کرن لڑائیاں

عشوے غمزے ناز نہورے
نخرے نوکاں ٹوکاں
حسن ملاحت شکل شباہت
ساریاں طرحیں سدھائیاں

ہنجڑوں جاری تتلے رتڑے
پیلیاں اجڑیاں پجڑیاں
لوکاں لیکھے اکھیں آئیاں
ظالم برہوں چنبھائیاں

میینیں سٹھڑیں درد اندیشے
ڈکھڑے پکھڑے آئم
دلڑی سختی ملڑی سنجڑی
اوکھیاں یاریاں لائیاں

مفت ملامت سخت ندامت
شہر شکایت چایم
ویڑھے یار فرید نہ آئم
مستک لکھیاں پائیاں

21 What Painful Love Is This?

What painful love is this I've gained,
From which sharp pain alone's obtained?

This is no love, but raging fire,
Consuming every part.
In burning grief and aching sighs
My life has been contained.

I have no confidante or friend,
And none to share my woes.
My love's unrivalled pain has made
My parents foes ingrained.

My clansfolk all know well that I
Yearn only for his tents.
My closest friends may criticize,
But I am unrestrained.

In all the city's streets and shops
The people show their scorn.
But thoughts of shame I've cast aside,
By young and old disdained.

This is no recent suffering,
But was so from the first:
And for my Nameless lover's sake
No name have I maintained.

I thread the garland of my tears,
And sit bewailing fate.
I know no way except for love,
In place of life attained.

21

کیا ڈکھڑا نینھ لہیوسے
ڈکھ باجھ پلے نہ پیوسے

عشق نہیں ہے نار غضب دی
تن من کیتس کولے
سولاں سٹرویں آہیں بھردے
ساری عمر نبھیوسے

نا غم خوار نہ کوئی ساتھی
نہ کوئی حال ونڈاوے
عشق جیہا ڈکھ ہور نہ کوئی
ما پیو ویری تھیوسے

خویش قبیلہ ہر کوئی جانے
منزل یار دیاں جھوکاں
سینگیاں سرتیاں کردیاں ٹوکاں
سارا بھرم لڑھیوسے

گلیاں کوچے شہر بزاراں
لوگ مریندا کانے
نندھڑے وڈڑے ڈیون طعنے
شرم شعور ونجیوسے

گالھ نہیں اج کل دی سنجڑی
روز ازل دی منٹھڑی
بے نشان سجن دے کیتے
نام نشان گنویوسے

ہار ہنجوں دا گل وچ پاواں
بیٹھی رو رو حال ونجاواں
پیت سوا ہئی ریت نہ کائی
ڈے سر مفت گدھیوسے

A double portion of distress
Was written in my fate.
And by my tears, now that he's left
Farid, the world is pained.

مونجھ منجھاری درد وچھوڑا
لکھیا باب تتی دے ڈوڑا
یار فرید خرید نہ کیتا
رو رو خلق رویوسے

22 Sorrow-Struck I Grieve

To mourn and keen is all
The love that I achieve.

Lacking you, my groom, oh!
Burning fills my breast, oh!
Cut to the heart, for home
Hatred I conceive.

Throbbing is my heart, oh!
Punnal makes it ache, oh!
Maybe he'll come again?
Sorrow-struck I grieve.

Darling of my heart, oh!
How untrue you proved, oh!
Whom now should I reproach?
He my love did leave.

How shall I describe, oh!
What is in my heart, oh!
Two-faced, these folk around
Sorely me aggrieve.

You my love perverse, oh!
Broke your faith with me, oh!
Leaving my life for nought
With regrets I heave.

My desire for him, oh!
Will not let me rest, oh!
Tangled am I with him
Who did me deceive.

22

سے سے سول سیاپے
ڈکھڑا نینسڑا لایم

توں بن گھر ور وے
ہاں دا ساڑا وے
سینے لکھ لکھ کاپے
ویڑھا کھاون آیم

پل پل دل نوں وے
پور پنل دے وے
ول آوے تاں جاپے
دردیں مار منجھایم

یار دلیں دے وے
پیت نہ پالی وے
کینوں ڈیواں ڈراپے
یاری تروڑ سدھایم

کیویں دل دا وے
حال سناواں وے
لوک سمجھے ڈچاچے
سختی سخت ستایم

یار اویڑے وے
توڑ نہ نبتی وے
جی جکھ جکھ پرتاپے
مفتی جان گوایم

سک ساجن دی وے
رہن نہ ڈیندی وے
جیں سنگ دلڑی اڑا
جیندے ناز مسایم

If my dark love comes, oh!
Into this my court, oh!
Gracious perhaps he'll be—
To this hope I cleave.

انگن فرید دے وے
سانول اوسی وے
کگم کریم آپے
تانگھیں آس ودھایم

23 I'm Lost

Without my beloved I'm lost
Without him what can I attain?

My darling has gone with his tents
And parting is all I obtain.

I'm tortured and racked by distress
How could you be so inhumane?

This courtyard oppresses my heart
I burn in a furnace of pain.

Uncaring of honour or shame
I wander through alley and lane.

From love I'll got sorrows untold
It's best that I soon should be slain.

23

ماہی باجھ کللیاں
دلدار بغیر اولیاں

ماہی جھوک لڈائی ویندا
سائنگ ہجر دے رلیاں

ترس نہ آوے ہک تل تینوں
سخت غماں وچ گلیاں

ویڑھا کھاوے انگن نہ بھاوے
اگ فراق دی جلیاں

شرم ونجایم بھرم گنوایم
رلدی کوچے گلیاں

عشق فرید بہوں ڈکھ ڈیسم
اج کل موئی موئی بھلیاں

24 Your Love Will I Bear Yet

Your love will I bear yet:
Shall any me upset?

I'll gladly sacrifice my life
And bear this burning ache.
I'll care no more for honour, but
All taunts will meekly take.
For his are all I am and own,
Apart though he me set.

In me consumed by love and pain
Are set confusion's tents:
I suffer ever sick distress.
My jewelled ornaments,
My quilts and former luxury—
All these I now forget.

My parents and my in-laws too
Contemn me, mock and jeer.
Yet still in this my deep distress
Towards his camp I veer,
Though all my tribe should jostle me
And make their violent threat.

Beneath his eyes' enchanting art
All sense and ease withdraw.
The grief which is my sorry fate
Unceasingly grows more.
His glances with their charging gaze
Me furiously beset.

24

تیرا نینہ نبھیساں زورے
سانوں منکے کون تے ہوڑے

جاں جلیساں سمیں سڑیساں
سمجھوں سوز سہیساں
سارا شرم لڑھیساں
ساری عار ویار اٹھیساں
تن من دھن سبھ ملک سجن دے
تونے کیجو کرم وچھوڑے

عشق اجاڑیم سولاں ساڑیم
درداں لائے دیرے
روگ کروپ کشالے ہر دم
گانے گہنے سہرے
راج ببانے تول وہانے
وسرے زورے تورے

پیکے ڈوکاں کرم سریجے
مارم جگتاں نوکاں
منٹھڑی دلڑی لٹڑی دا
ہے قبلہ یار دیاں جھوکاں
ما پیو خویش قبیلہ مل مل
ڈینندے دھکڑے دھوڑے

چشماں جادو جوڑ جگائے
ہوش قرار بھلایا
ڈکھڑے پکھڑے آئے غم ہم
دم دم نال سوایا
غمزے خوب دھموڑے ڈیون
رمزاں گھتدیاں گھوڑے

My darling can I not forget,
But crying in distress,
In life or death and weal or woe
My love shall I profess,
Although through doubly stabbing pain
I double sorrows get.

یار فرید نہ وسرم ہرگز
رو رو دھانہیں کر ساں
جیندیں مردیں او کھیں سوکھیں
ساہ محبت بھر ساں
دوہری سکدی سانگ جگر وچ
جے ڈکھ ڈیوم ڈوڑے

25 The Omens Parting Prophesy

The omens parting prophesy—
I fear my love will not come nigh.

Now joys are few and hardship's grown,
While grief with pain together's thrown:
The spinning-wheel creaks out its drone,
The twisted thread in spun awry.

My henna's dim, my parting's wrong,
My kohl and lipstick gone since long:
With all hope lost despair is strong—
My every pore shrieks out its cry.

These quilts and pillows sorely press
These threaded wreaths of flowers oppress:
These halls now seem a wilderness—
And all my anguish multiply.

Sad days are here, and luck is missed—
Forlorn I wait with bangled wrist:
Alive may I with him keep tryst,
For otherwise I'll surely die!

My bracelets and my anklets break,
My ornaments to bits I shake,
My necklace seems to me a snake,
My pointed beads sharp stabs supply.

My Ranjha dear I cannot see,
Who left me sad and solitary:
The griefs around my neck to me
All patience and repose deny.

25

اج فال فراق ڈسیندی ہے
متاں یار کنوں تکھڑیندی ہے

سختیاں ودھیاں سکھ تھیئے تھولے
رنج و الم غم سوز سمولے
چرخا ڈکھڑی روں روں بولے
تند ڈنگی ول پیندی ہے

سیندھاں کجڑیاں میندیاں پھکڑیاں
کجلے اجڑے سرخیاں بکھڑیاں
یاساں ملیاں آساں تکھڑیاں
لوں لوں وین ولیندی ہے

تول نہالیاں دار ڈسیجن
ہار پھلاں دے خار ڈسیجن
صحن حویلیاں بار ڈسیجن
سب شے مونجھ ودھیندی ہے

بھاگ گیا بد بختی جاگی
بانہہ چڑیلی تھیوم ڈوہاگی
جیندیں ڈیکھاں سانول ساگی
جندڑی مر مر ویندی ہے

ٹوٹے کنگن کڑیاں نیور
ٹکڑے بیڑے بولے پینسر
کٹمالے تھیئے نانگ برابر
چوہنب کلی چک پیندی ہے

نظر نہ آوے رانجھن ماہی
کیتس بے کس تے بےواہی
مونجھ منجھاری گل دی پھاہی
صبر ارام ونجھیندی ہے

With pale and mottled cheeks I rue,
My shirt is black, my shawl is blue:
How ill my state is, lacking you—
While folk their mocking taunts let fly.

That nuptial joy to sorrow veers,
No way to be with him appears:
These wretched eyes are tired of tears,
My heart gives forth its bitter sigh.

Now March's spring is turned to fall
And on these tents lies ruin's pall:
I see no remedy at all—
These sands, like witches, terrify.

My love stayed not to bid farewell
And parting's load upon me fell:
With yearning does my bosom swell,
Through cruel fate no ease have I.

درد کنوں منہ ساوا پیلا
چولا کالا بوچھن نیلا
توں بن ساڈا کوجھا حیلہ
ہر کئی سخت الیندی ہے

سون شگون سبھے تھئے پتھرے
وصل وصال دے سانگے ترٹرے
نین نہ بھائے رو رو ہٹرے
دلڑی کیس کریندی ہے

چیتر بہار خزاں ڈسیجے
جھوک سبھو ویران ڈسیجے
نا کوئی علم نا بان ڈسیجے
روہی ڈین ڈریندی ہے

یار فرید نہ کھڑ مکلایا
باری بار ہجر سر آیا
سک سڑیا تے تانگھاں تایا
قسمت رودھے ڈیندی ہے

26 May He Come

Thanks to you, my Ranjha dear,
Ill-fortune over me is spread.

My life is spent among old maids,
Unable truly to be wed.

I've cords of grief on wrists and feet,
And sorrow's shawl upon my head.

My home and in-laws are my foes
My friends their quarrel will not shed.

Come now to me and hold me tight,
Beloved, lying on my bed.

I suffer blows upon my breast:
Through countless wounds my heart has bled.

Wipe out this grievous fate, O Lord!
Ah may he come before I'm dead!

26

درد پۓ ول پییۓ
ڈٹرے یار رٹچھٹے

میں بیٹھیں گئی عمر نہ آئے
لانویں لہن دے نیٹے

ہتھڑیں پیریں غم دے گانے
سر سولاں دے ریٹے

سینگلیں سرتیں لگڑے جھیڑے
سکڑیں سورھیں پھٹے

سانول آوے آگل لاوے
سہجوں سینچھیں لیٹے

دلڑے سو سو زخم کللڑے
سینے سخت چیسٹے

یار فرید سنبھالم جیندیں
رب ڈکھ ڈکھڑے مٹے

27 My Heart Is But A Pawn

My heart is but a pawn
Of my shepherd swain.

Stay always near, and like a charm
That o'er the heart is worn
Your sweet embrace I will maintain.

On me who've pined the whole night through
Has burst the light of dawn.
To hug me why do you disdain?

With Savan's gentle clouds and showers
Our meeting near has drawn.
This passion gives me nought but pain.

If grief I heave my bitter sighs,
Immersed in tears I mourn
And from my dress I swell and strain.

To poor Farid you prove untrue—
Though you to come had sworn,
My love, you have not come again.

27

مان مہیں دا چاک

اساڈے من بھاوندا

ہر دم ہوویں کولے میڈے

کر رکھاں دل پاک

وتاں گلگکڑی پاوندا

راتیں روندی پٹدیں کھپدیں

پھٹ گئی ہم باکھ

کیوں گل نہیں لاوندا

سانون سمجوں مینگھ ملھاراں

آئی ملن دی مد ساکھ

نیسڑا جیڑا تاوندا

دردوں ٹھڈڑیاں ساہیں کڈھدی

رو رو ڈیواں باک

ڈکھڑا انگ نہ ماوندا

نال فرید دے سچ نہ کیتو

آون دی گیوں آکھ

سوہنا ول نہیں آوندا

28 Rano End My Pain

Sweet Rano, leave the Kak
And end tonight my pain.

It was for love of you that I
Did sleep with Sumal feign.

If only for a week or so
In this my hall remain.

Would they consider in Marwar
What you have done humane?

Besides the Kak let us enjoy
Together Savan's rain.

What grudge have you that now no more
To look at me you deign?

These sufferings untold how should
My single mouth explain?

I'll feed you sugar-cakes, my crow—
Just say we'll meet again.

Oh what a giver, what a gift!
Through passion grief I gain.

From day to night, from night to dawn
My weeping I maintain.

Despair and anguish from the first
This love did foreordain.

28

میڈا مٹھڑا مانہوں کاک جا
شالا راناں ایندم رات

تیڈی سک دے کان ستی ہم
سومل کوں گھن سات

پھیر سہائیں جیندیں ماڑیاں
توئے ڈینہ پچھے سات

سچ ڈس جو کجھ کیتی ایہا
ماڑدی ھئی مرجات

کاک کندھن تے رل مل مانوں
ساون دی برسات

کہیں وٹڑی وہ گیو ہاں تے
ول نہ پایو جھات

غم دا حال سناواں کیویں
سو ڈکھ تے ہک وات

کانگل کھنڈ دیاں چوریاں ڈیساں
کر کئی ملن دی بات

پیت پٹھے نت درد کشالے
واہ ڈاتے دی ڈات

ڈینھ گھنے رو راتیں کیتم
راتیں کئی پربھات

مونجھ ملال فرید ملیوسے
ازلوں برہوں برات

29 Leaving Me Distraught

Oh leaving me distraught, my love
With whom do you consort, my love?

Baloch beloved, Kech's heir
You have reduced me to despair
And to these mountains brought, my love.

You took your tents to far Malhir
Alone with strangers left me here
Without an afterthought, my love.

Oh silly me, how could I gauge
How fierce this wolf-like love would rage,
When first your eyes mine sought, my love?

You made me love you, so alone
Why have you with your camels flown,
Misled by false report, my love?

Through you I'm in this wretched plight—
See now, you have consumed me quite
To ash in grief's retort, my love.

Oh you it was who reached Bhambhor
Professed your love then came no more
Deceiving me for nought, my love.

When will he think of me at all,
To sit beside him gently call?
I need my luck's support, my love.

29

اساں کنوں دل چایو وے یار
جاپے کتھاں وچ لایو

یار برو چل کیچ دا والی
کیتو حال کنوں بے حالی
پربت روہ رلایو وے یار

ملک ملھیر لتونی جھوکاں
میں کلھڑی وچ اوپریاں لوکاں
ہک تل ترس نہ آیو وے یار

میں کملی کیا جاناں نینھہ کوں
ظلمی نہر تے قہری شینھہ کوں
آپے دید اڑایو وے یار

آپے اپنا سوہاں کیتو
کرہوں قطاریو نال نہ نیتو
کیں دھوتی برمایو وے یار

یار مٹھی کوں ڈتڑو رولا
ساڑیو کیتو کیری کولا
تتڑی کوں کیوں تایو وے یار

آپے شہر بھنبھور ڈو آیوں
یاری لاکر چھوڑ سدھایوں
مفتا کوڑ کمایو وے یار

یار فرید کڈاں سنبھلیسی
سہجوں سڈ کر کول بلھیسی
جے وت بخت بھڑایو وے یار

30 My Thoughts To Whom Should I Confide?

My thoughts to whom should I confide?
All friendly ears am I denied.

With dust and ashes on my head
All shame and honour have I shed:
None comes to care for me—instead
Me all with mocking laughs deride.

By passion's burden overweighed
The butt of public scorn I'm made:
Unceasing tears my life pervade—
No token of my goal I've spied.

My heart for you, beloved, moans,
In agony it writhes and groans:
Distress and grief alone it owns—
Thus dwells with scarce a heart your bride!

Whole teams of doctors diagnose
And medicines for my ills propose:
And yet, since none my secret knows,
I feel no change at all inside.

To bid farewell he would not say:
To Kech my Punnal stole away
With full intent, and dared to stay
It was because I slept—but lied!

Hear, Laila, how your poor Majnun
With heartfelt cries does importune
His fair beloved, 'Lift up soon
The curtain from your litter's side!'

30

کیا حال سناواں دل دا
کوئی محرم راز نہ ملدا

منھ دھوڑ مٹی سر پایم
سارا ننگ نموز ونجایم
کوئی پچھن نہ ویہڑے آیم
ہتھوں الٹا عالم کھلدا

آیا بار برہوں سر باری
لگی ہو ہو شہر خواری
روندیں عمر گزاریم ساری
نہ پایم ڈس منزل دا

دل یار کنتے کرلاوے
تڑپھاوے تے غم کھاوے
ڈکھ پاوے سول نبھاوے
ایہو طور تیڈے بیدل دا

کئی سہنس طبیب کہاون
سے پڑیاں جھول پلاون
میڈے دل دا بھید نہ پاون
پووے فرق نہیں ہک تل دا

پنوں ہوت نہ کھڑ مکلایا
چھڈ کلھڑی کیچ سدھایا
سوہنے جان چھچان رلایا
کوڑا عذر نبھایم گھل دا

سن لیلیٰ دھانتھ پکارے
تیڈا مجنوں زار نزارے
سوہنا یار تونے ہکوارے
کڈیں چا پردہ محمل دا

My heart now for love's city yearns,
But how the way there twists and turns!
Farid no road or pass discerns—
What hardships will this route provide!

دل پریم نگر ڈوں تاگھے

جتھاں پینڈے سخت اڑانگے

ناراہ فرید نہ لانگھے

ہے پندھ بہوں مشکل دا

31 I Seek The Wilderness's Air

I cannot stay my restless heart,
But seek the wilderness's air:
My tribesman's grievous love has set
Me wandering in the desert bare.

What then of woe am I to say?
My heart is pained by night and day.
O God, behold my state, I pray—
How I lie helpless in despair.

To me has fate no kindness shown:
My heart is all to anguish prone,
My lover not one glance has thrown—
To my distress no end is there.

Since we together had such fun
With home and husband's home I'm done,
And in my madness all I shun:
For no one have I any care.

Continually my heart-ache grows,
Increasing are my cruel woes,
While only grief rejoicing knows—
Such is my fortune, I declare.

My days their double care provide,
Both anxiousness and pain beside,
Until I grieve at eventide,
'He comes not, still quite unaware.'

31

دلے دارم بسے آوارہ
طبعے وحشت آرائے
برہوں ہارے بروچل دے
بیاباں دشت رلوائے

کہاں غم دیاں کیہاں باتیں
ڈکھی ہے دل ڈیہاں راتیں
خدا را حال زارم بیں
کہ بے دستنیم و بے پائے

بما طالع شدہ پر کیں
نزارم بے دل و غمگیں
نہ پیندا یار ہے چھاتی
اجن ڈکھڑے نہ پاندائے

سجن وس رس ڈکھایم چس
سر سمجھیں پیکڑیں بس بس
دل دیوانہ با ہر کس
نہ دارد ہیچ پروائے

ہمیشہ مونجھ وادھی ہے
سنجی سختی زیادی ہے
سدا سولاں دی شادی ہے
میں اپنے بخت ازمائے

ڈیہاں ڈوری خرابی ہے
قلق ہے اضطرابی ہے
نماشاں جی عذابی ہے
نہ آپ آئے نہ بلوائے

These fevered cheeks my passions show,
While in my heart since long ago
These wounds like scarlet poppies glow—
Oh let me see him, anywhere!

Let claims no other institute,
For me alone, Farid, these suit—
The countless pains, the painful route
Past shades of demon, witch, and bear.

ز عشق عارض رنگیں
چولا لہ داغ ہا دیریں
کیتیاں ہن دل اندر جاہیں
کڈیں رب یار ملوائے

بغیر از من کرا شاید
فرید ایں مرمرا باید
ڈکھے پینڈے تے ڈکھ بے حد
ممیں راہِس تے رچھ سائے

32 How Strange Is Passion's Pain

How strange is passion's pain!
With inner griefs untold I fret,
My eyes their water rain,
While in my heart my wounds are wet.

Through ill-accord from love resulting
I must endure my kin's insulting:
I am my parents' bane,
By hostile countrymen beset.

Now stabbed by cruel spears of parting
With burning love my heart is smarting:
My body cleft in twain
Displays his skilful dart's effect.

His magic glances quite enthral me,
His eyes with robber-looks now maul me:
His cruel tresses' skein
Entwines me in its twisted net.

For Punnal in unceasing yearning
I bear the Maru desert's burning,
Most sorely vexed by pain:
I must do that on which I'm set.

Soft bedclothes hurt me now like witches,
I've put aside all ease and riches:
Each part of me is slain
By passion's blade and bayonet.

My love to me no more approaches,
Grief's camp upon my thoughts encroaches:
This burning frame and brain
I surely shall bear grave-wards yet.

32

عشق انوکھڑی پیڑ
سو سو سول اندر دے
نین وہاون نیر
الڑے زخم جگر دے

برہوں بکھیڑا سخت اویڑا
خویش قبیلہ لاوم جھیڑا
مارم ما پیو ویر
دشمن لوک شہر دے

تانگ اولڑا سانگ کلکلڑی
جندڑی جلڑی دلڑی گلڑی
تن من دے وچ تیر
مارے یار ہنر دے

غمزے سحری رمزاں ویری
اکھیاں جادو دید لٹیری
ظلمیں زلف زنجیر
پیچی پیچ قہر دے

پیت پنل دی سک پل پل دی
ماروتھل دی ریت پچھلدی
ڈکھ لاوم تر بھیڑ
جو سر دے سو کر دے

تول نہالی ڈین ڈکھالی
صبر ارام دی وسریم چالی
لوں لوں لکھ لکھ چیر
کاری تیغ تبر دے

یار فرید نہ پایم پھیرا
لایا درداں دل وچ دیرا
سر گیوم سہیس سریر
نیساں داغ قبر دے

33 I'll Bear This Passion's Ache

For whom then did you go
And me alone forsake?

How pitilessly you
Did thrust in parting's stake!

Yet of the Thal entire
A single leap I'll make.

So long as I draw breath
I'll bear this passion's ache.

With call to grief did love
Me newly-born awake.

Confound this love! Let me
Be bitten by some snake!

So young I was when I
Was branded for your sake.

Am I so rare? See those
Whom love before did take.

Amidst these shoals, Farid,
I see no ford or stake.

33

میکوں کھڑا چھوڑ تے
ویندی کیندے سانگ

قطرہ محض لکیس نہ آیو
لایو ہجر دی سانگ

تھل مارو دا پینڈا سارا
تھیسم ہک بلھانگ

جے تنیں ناسیں دے وچ ساہم
رہسم تیڈڑی تانگ

جاون لادی برہوں سنایم
کنیں ڈھان دی بانگ

صدقے کہتے ہیں نینھ کولہوں
کھاوم کالڑے نانگ

چھوٹے وقت کوارے ویلے
لگڑم تیڈڑا دانگ

میں ہاں کیرڑھے باغ دی مولی
کئی رل موئے میں وانگ

گھمر گھیر فرید کپردے
نہ تڑ ڈسم نہ ٹانگ

34 My Thoughts On Ranjha's Land Are Bent

Afire with burning languishment
My thoughts on Ranjha's land are bent.

In telling parting's ugly tale
My breath is caught, my heart is rent.

With blistered feet must I endure
The twisting mountain-path's ascent.

With crippled heart and heavy pain
I struggle in bewilderment.

May God remove this weight of grief
And let me see in life his tent.

Distraction, sorrow, sickness, woe—
These four by love as gifts are sent.

Those beauties' way has ever been
Deceit and false inveiglement.

He may or may not care for me—
My heart is still on him intent.

34

سک ساڑے تانگ پچالے
وطن نہ وسرم رانجھن والے

ہجر فراق دا کوجھا قصہ
ساہ منجھائے تے ہاں ڈالے

راہ اولڑے لکھ لکھ ولڑے
ڈونگر کالے پیریں چھالے

دلڑی جدڑی ڈکھڑیں لڈڑی
کینویں ہوش حواس سنبھالے

جیندیں ڈیکھاں جھوک سجن دی
قادر بار غماں دے ٹالے

عشق سوغاتاں میں ول بھیجیاں
درد اندیشے روگ کشالے

ہے سوہنیاں دی عادت اصلوں
کُوڑے پیچ فریبی چالے

یار فرید نہ اترم دل توں
لطفوں بھالے خواہ نہ بھالے

35 Go Now And Be His

Now my love is come
Gone are sorrows all.

Go now and be his
Burn your bed and shawl.

Serve your love alone
Be his slave and thrall.

Come now in your heart
Him alone instal.

True to love I die
Punnal, bear my pall.

'Travel to the sands!'
Is my yearning call.

35

اجھو مارو ملیو
دل نہ ماندی تھی

سوہے سیج کوں ساڑ تے
ونج مِتراں دی تھی

باندی بردی یار دی
بردی باندی تھی

غیروں الفت یار دے
دلڑی واندی تھی

نینھ نبھیندیں مر گیوم
پنل کاندھی تھی

تانگھ فرید نوں آکھدی
بر ڈوں پاندھی تھی

Part III

Songs of the Desert and the Rains

The poems in this final section include many of those by which Khwaja Farid is best remembered. Often unique of their kind individually, they collectively serve to establish the character and stature of his poetic originality.

In '*Drive gently*', for instance, the heroine through whom the poet speaks is imagined as being driven through the desert, rather than helplessly stumbling. The conventional theme of Sassi's desperate desert-journey in search of Punnun does, however, serve as the basis of the next poems, where the terrors of the sands are described in the most evocative way, first simply and poignantly in '*In these far desert ways*', at greater length in '*My death would be no heaviness*', then with an extraordinary rhetorical elaboration of imagery in the splendid '*Where the desert-grasses twist*'. The all-embracing quality of Khwaja Farid's poetic art is well illustrated by the contrast between this poem and the following '*The ways of love stretch far indeed*', where the motif of the desert home is intertwined with reference to that other desert of Karbala and with the imagery of the Sufi ghazal.

The songs of the rains begin with the rather conventional Braj poem '*Savan's rains*'. But is was the spectacle of the desert in the rains which called forth many of the Khwaja's most vivid lyrics, as is well illustrated in '*I'll not stop here*', with its long and resonant meter. '*The rain-clouds of July*' evokes the beauties of nature during the rains in a series of striking images, more simply expressed in '*The east wind blows*', but elaborated to the most magnificent effect in '*Savan's happy days*'.

The last five poems all derive from Khwaja Farid's fascination with the life of the nomadic tribesmen of the desert, and most seem to relate to his romantic association with the desert-girl Haram Mai Hotan. '*Go fetch me some bracelets*' is an unusual handling of a folk-song motif.

The famous poem '*The nomad-maids*' really speaks for itself. '*Our reservoir*' is one of a small group of poems connected with the practice of digging holes in the desert to catch the water of the rains, and a similar scene is evoked by the closely associated '*Let's build a booth*', equally remarkable for its rhyme. The last poem of all is '*The Pilu-pickers*', the lengthy description of the scene witnessed or imagined during the harvest of the pilu-berries, the small fruit of the jal-tree. This is far the best-known of all Khwaja Farid's poems, quite without parallel in his own works or those of his predecessors, and has a peculiar magic all its own.

36 Drive Gently

Drive gently this my chariot!

Break not these crystal bangles fine
Which on my wrists are set.

No jolting carriage can I bear:
I'm easily upset.

About my shoulders from the first
Was cast your passion's net.

Safe with my load may I traverse
This route by thieves beset.

If riding in this car I tire
A chestnut horse I'll get—

Not headstrong, one who's led with ease,
A swift and gentle pet.

With Ranjha was I put by God:
We form a perfect set.

In yearning for his sight, fresh pains
My bosom daily fret.

Drive on! These twisting paths my heart
With fresh impatience whet.

We shall, Farid, there in Bhambhor
Enjoy each other yet.

36

رتھ دھیمیں دھیمیں ٹور

میڈا دستہ نرم کرور دا
متاں ونگیں لگم نکور

رتھ تے بہندی ڈرک نہ سہندی
ہم طبع کمزور

روز ازل دی پاتم گل وچ
برہوں تیڈے دی ڈور

شالہ مولھ سلامت نیواں
راہ وچ لڑدن چور

جیکر رتھ بیٹھیں تھک پوساں
گھوڑا گھنساں بور

سوکھا تیز لگام دا کولا
نا اوکھا سر زور

رانجھن تے میں جوڑ کوں جوڑوں
جوڑ جوڑیندا جوڑ

سک تے طلب ملن دی سینے
روز نواں ہم شور

پندھ اڑانگے دلڑی تانگھے
جلد پچاویں توڑ

میں تے یار فرید منیسوں
رل مل شہر بھنبھور

37 In These Far Desert Ways

My Hot has gone and left
Our old togetherness, sir.

Of him I see no sign:
No goal can I define,
Nor anywhere to rest, sir.

In these far desert ways
And mountains' rocky maze
I call without success, sir.

Along these paths so sore
The bears and rhinos roar,
While I'm left succourless, sir.

The clustered demon apes,
The bog that widely gapes
My every step arrest, sir.

Distress torments me ill
And roasts me on its grill,
To gnaw my bones and flesh, sir.

37

ساری عمر گزاریم گڈ سائیں
ہن ہوت پنل گیوم لڈ سائیں

نہ کل یار سجن دی
نہ رہ گئی جوہ جتن دی
نہ تر تاڈے مڈ سائیں

تھل مارو دیاں پٹیاں
ڈونگر اوکھیاں گھٹیاں
اپڑم توڑ نہ سڈ سائیں

سخت اویڑے پینڈے
رڑدے رچھ تے گینڈے
اٹھ گئی آس تے تنڈ سائیں

باندر راکھس گھاٹے
کھڑ بن کھوب گپاٹے
قدم قدم تے کھڈ سائیں

درد فرید ستاوے
اگ لاوے بھن کھاوے
پٹ پٹ ماس تے ہڈ سائیں

38 My Death Would Be No Heaviness

I hate this dreadful love of mine:
My death would be no heaviness—ah me!

Since to Malhir he cruelly went
No message here to me he's sent:
I wander now in shamelessness—ah me!

That he had gone I did not know:
My useless life is spent in woe—
My lover gives me no redress—ah me!

My fated sorrows multiply,
Those huts are razed, those pools are dry—
My heart is struck by sore distress—ah me!

The mountain-passes' thorns and stones,
The Maru desert's frightful zones
I suffer, but without success—ah me!

The burning sands my feet abuse,
My blisters trail their glittering ooze,
But all I gain is wretchedness—ah me!

I struggle through the hilly land,
By grievous paths dunes of sand—
Behold his tender tenderness—ah me!

My love has not been kind, Farid!
Alas, ill-fortune has decreed
That I be left here loverlesss—ah me!

38

نینھ نہ بھایا سخت برا ہے
بار اجل سر باری بھلو

مارو محب ملھیر سدھایا
ولدا کوئی پیغام نہ آیا
پھر دی شہر اواری بھلو

کیچ گیاں دی خبر نہ آئی
روندیں گل گئی عمر اجائی
یار نہ کیتم کاری بھلو

ڈکھڑے ڈکھڑے آیم پکھڑے
تاڈے ڈھٹڑے ٹوبھے سکڑے
دلڑی دردیں ماری بھلو

سکرے کنڈڑے راہ جبل دے
اوکھے پینڈے مارو تھل دے
سولیں ساڑی ہاری بھلو

ریت تھلاں دی پیر بچالے
جھلکن چھلکن لکھ لکھ چھالے
پلڑے پیوم خواری بھلو

روہ ڈونگر دیاں اوکھیاں گھٹیاں
مارو تھل دیاں ڈکھڑیاں پٹیاں
وہ وہ یار دی یاری بھلو

عشق فرید نہ کیتم بھلا
ہے ہے بخت نہ تھیوم سولا
ویندم ہوت وساری بھلو

39 Where The Desert-Grasses Twist

Where the desert-grasses twist, my love
Ever-shifting shapes exist, my love.

The crickets creak, the pigeons coo
The foxes howl, hyenas new
The geckoes puff, the lizards whoo
The snakes and serpents hiss, my love.

In these fair mounds and hills of sand
These graceful stones, this gravel bland,
Ravines and tanks and gullies grand
The rains all grief dismiss, my love.

These thorns and splinters prick me sore—
They too are signs of love, I'm sure:
The blood which from my wounds does pour
A wedding-mark I wist, my love.

I'll suffer as my joyful art
The fire of grief and passion's smart.
My wounds bleed like my wounded heart—
These are your painful gift, my love.

Oh, in this desert's blessed sight
I'll die indeed, but not take fright,
Though through your cruel heart by night
And day I'm feverish, my love.

Since her Baloch his campment tore
So sadly distant from Bhambhor
Her own heart's bleeding gobbets raw
Are Sassi's dreadful grist, my love.

39

جتھ تھلڑا جتھ دربوں ہے یار
اتھ ہر ویلے لدبوں ہے یار

تنڈڑے چیکن گیرے گھوکن
جرکھاں ترکھاں لومبڑ کوکن
گوہیں شوکن سانٹھے پھوکن
نانگیں دی شوں شوں ہے یار

سوہنیاں ٹھیڑیاں ٹبرے بھٹڑے
نازو والے نکڑے وٹڑے
باہیں ٹوبھے پاڑے گھٹڑے
وٹھڑیں ڈکھڑا ووں ہے یار

کنڈڑیں کاٹھیں نشتر ماری
سمجھوں یاری تے غمخواری
الڑی پھٹڑیں توں رت جاری
خاص سہاگ دی پوں ہے یار

ہن کھل ہاسے ساڈے پیٹھے
سول سڑاپے درد اندیشے
زیرے زخم تے زخمیں ریشے
سب ڈکھ ڈٹڑا توں ہے یار

روہی محض بشارت درسوں
مرسوں بھرسوں مول نہ ڈرسوں
بے درداں دی دلڑی ترسوں
ڈینھ راتیں گھوں موں ہے یار

جیں ڈینھ ہوت نیتے پٹ دیرے
شہر بھنبھوروں سخت پریرے
دل دیاں بوٹیاں ہاں دے بیرے
سسّی دی موں موں ہے یار

Without you, dear, what life is there?
What am I left with but despair?
Just poison lies, to you I swear,
In every cup and dish, my love.

توں بن یار فرید دا جیون
جیندیں جگ وچ ڈکھڑا تھیون
زہر ڈسیوے کھاون پیون
تیڈے سر دی سوں ہے یار

40 The Ways Of Love Stretch Far Indeed

Oh listen, clever expert friend,
The ways of love stretch far indeed.

For death's fell sword no care have I
Though destiny its dart lets fly,
For in your look my death I read.

'If fortune's kind then friends are too'[1]
Perversely, then why should not you
Be with my fate on spite agreed?

Our joy it is to weep and wail
Our town the desert's lonely vale
Muharram's mourning is our Id.

The travellers bring news of rain
Of how the desert blooms again
Where countless flocks their shepherds lead.

My soul in held by smart and pain
My heart is gripped by passions plain[2]
I see my rival as Yazid.

Your prayer-mat and robes destroy
To wash your soul pure wine employ—
For so the Magian priest decreed.

My dark beloved's look cajole
And with his strut and sable mole
Have freely quite enslaved Farid.

---

[1]   A proverb.

[2]   Or 'passion's plain', i.e. the pain of Karbala.

40

سن وو سہیلی سگھڑ سیانی
برہوں دے پندھڑے سخت بعید

نا کل میکوں تیغ قضا دی
نا تقدیر دے تیر وغا دی
کیتم دوست دی دید شہید

جے ڈینھ بھلڑے متر وی بھلڑے
قسمت جوڑے جوڑ کلڑے
یار شدید تے بخت عنید

روون پٹن کوں سمجھوں شادی
سنج بر جھر جھنگ ڈسم آبادی
عشرہ محرم ساڈڑی عید

سو سو چھانگاں لکھ لکھ چھیڑو
وٹھڑے دی ووہ ڈیون پندھیڑو
روہی تھئی آباد جدید

جند اسیر اے جور و جفا دی
دلڑی قیدی کرب و بلا دی
ڈسم رقیب یزید پلید

سٹ خرقہ بھٹ گھت سجادہ
جامۂ جاں شو پاک ببادا
کردم پیر مغاں تاکید

سانول یار دے ناز نگہ دے
مارو چال تے خال سیہ دے
تھیوسے مفت فرید خرید

41 Savan's Rains

Now Savan's rains the earth bedew.

You further fire my burning heart,
Confounded rainbird, with your coo.

The cuckoo, crane, and peacock cry
And fill my heart with sadness new.

My eyes keep strugling with repose,
While I keep tossing all night through.

With trembling heart my bosom shakes:
I fear these rain-clouds, lacking you.

The rains with their voluptuous joy
My body with delights endue.

Sad times are past, so to him go—
Say, 'Come now to my bed, oh do!'

My limbs in longing waste away—
My lover is to me untrue.

41

ساون بونڈڑیاں جھر لاوے

کوک کوک پاپی ٹرے پپیہا
پھوک پھوک تن آگ جگاوے

کوئل کونج مہروا بولے
دل دکھیاری نوں ڈکھ تاوے

نین چین سے جھگڑت جھگڑت
تڑپھت تڑپھت رین بہاوے

چھتیاں دھڑکت جیا را لرجت
ننج بن کاری گھٹن ڈراوے

روم جھوم رت برکھا سوہے
انگ ڈھنگ رس راند رچاوے

بیت گئے دن رین ڈکھاں دے
کہو ری پیا کو سیمجھ سہاوے

پیتم پیت فرید نہ پالی
انگ انگ برہن مرجھاوے

42 I'll Not Stop Here

Without you, love, for death alone I pray:
In life I will not for an instant stay.

Towards the east the gathering clouds I saw
And lightning's flash, and heard the thunder's roar:
I'll not stop here, but to your land away!

I catch the gentle sound of desert-rain—
No heed you pay me, love, whom grief has slain:
I rip my robes, held fast in frenzy's sway.

Desire to go back home my heart controls,
To see those grasses, camps, and waterholes:
Now to the sands I'll wend my sorry way.

To sound their crashing roll the clouds arise:
I call your name and utter helpless cries—
Unless I see you, now let death me slay!

My lipstick, henna, lines of kohl are wrecked,
My nose is bare of rings, my hair undecked:
My old toilette is turned to disarray.

Now vanished quite is all my stock of mirth,
And pain is all I gain in pleasure's dearth—
How well my love his spark of love did lay!

The lightning makes my heart our camp recall,
And from my eyes monsoons of tears now fall—
I cry and cry amidst this rain's display.

42

توں بن موت بھلی ویندم شالا مری
ٹکساں ہک نہ ذری جیساں پل نہ گھڑی

پورب طرف ڈھوں مینگھ ملہار ڈٹھم
بجلی لسک ڈٹی گج گج گاج سنیم
رہساں اتھ نہ اڑی ویسا وطن وری

کنڑیں ورڑ پیوم روہی وٹھڑی دی
ڈھولا کل نہ لدھو ڈکھڑیں کٹھڑی دی
پھڑیم چولی چنی رو رو تھیوم چری

اپنے دیس ونجاں دل نوں تانگھ تھئی
ڈیکھاں تاڈے ٹوبھے لانے کھار بوئی
برڈوں راہی تھیواں ساڑیں سول سڑی

اونگاں بونگ اٹھن بدلی کیتی لس
گھن گھن نام تیڈا روندی تھئی بے وس
سانول تینوں ملاں یا سر پیوم مری

سرخی مہندی مٹھی کجلا دھار گیوم
ناز نواز بھلیا ہار سنگار گیوم
یینسر بول بھناں اجڑی مانگھ دھڑی

کھیڈن کوڈن گیا سکھ دا ڈول گیوم
ڈکھڑے پکھڑے پئے خوشیاں رول گیم
جڑ کر راول جوگی لائی پرم جڑی

کمھدی کمھن فرید جھوکاں یاد پوون
اکھیاں نیر ہنجوں کر برسات وس
لکھ لکھ دھانٹھ اٹھم جاں جاں ڈسم جھٹری

43 The Rain-Clouds Of July

If you have pity, come, my love,
To watch the rain-clouds of July.

I sit to weep and watch the roads
And let my raven fly.

I seek the omens all night long:
By day I cast my die.

Without you, lord of Kech's land,
How harsh a life have I.

I wed you on the first of days—
So why now me deny?

The lonely dunes entrance my heart:
I bid the town goodbye.

That God has made Malhir to bloom
This spring does testify.

Now rivers from the pouring rain
Flow in the desert dry.

Blue, yellow, red, the rainbows glint
Like fish-scales in the sky.

The scarlet caper, bulrush white
The emerald alkali!

Before each hut the pots are churned
And sweet the cowbells cry.

43

ساون مینگھ ملھاراں
ترس پووی پنل آ موڑ مہاراں

ہنجڑوں ہاراں واٹ نہاراں
بیٹھی کانگ اڈاراں

سنجڑیاں راتیں پاواں فلاں
ڈینناں ڈھالے ماراں

توں بن کیچ شہر دا والی
اوکھی عمر گزاراں

روز ازل دیاں لدھیم لاواں
ہن کیوں کردیں عاراں

سنجڑیں ٹبڑیں دلڑی موہی
وسرے شہر بزاراں

ملک ملھیر وسایم مولا
تھیاں چو گوٹھ بہاراں

تھل چترانگ ڈسیجن ندیاں
رم جھم لاسوں تاراں

نیلیاں پیلیاں رتیاں پینگھاں
مچھلی سہنس ہزاراں

سرخ کریںٹھ تے چٹڑیاں بوٹیاں
ساویاں لانیاں کھاراں

جو پھر جو پھر گھبکن مٹیاں
سوہندیاں گھنڈ تواراں

The camels, cows, and goats and sheep
In lines to graze pass by.

I'll doff these dirty clothes, Farid,
Should he to me draw nigh.

گئیں بکریاں بھیڈاں چانگے
چردے جوڑ قطاراں

یار فرید ملم دل بھاندا
میلے ویس اتاراں

44 The East Wind Blows

My far-off love, the east wind blows!

The coming of the rains has made
Each desert-shrub a blooming rose.

The thunder's roar and lightning's flash
Fresh raptures to my heart disclose.

The waving grass upon the sands
A bridal canopy bestrows.

With water in the desert-pools
Towards the Indus now who goes?

With daily greater joy, Farid,
My heart more cheerful ever grows.

44

پردیسی یارا وا پورب دی گھلے

سانوں مینہ برسات دی واری
بھوگ پھلی کھپ پھلے

گاجاں لگن بجلیاں لسکن
ذوقوں دلڑی چلے

دھامن کترن سنگھ تے سنجھوں
چتر سہاگ دا جھلے

جے تیئں پانی پلھڑ نہ کھٹسی
کون بھلا سندھ جلے

روز بروز فرید ہے لذت
طبع ڈینھو ڈینھ کھلے

45 Savan's Happy Days

Savan's happy days are here—
How they fill my heart with ease!

These darkling clouds which come from far,
From east and south, and from Marwar,
These gusts from every quarter are
Of coming rains the prophecies.

The wild goose, the lark and hen,
The cuckoo, peacock and the wren,
The partridge and all birds again
Are busy with their melodies.

The rainbows green and gold by day,
By night the lightning's bright display,
And thunder's gently rumbling lay—
What times of happiness are these!

The barren deserts bloom again
And gardens blossom in the plain:
The cattle-bells and heavy rain
Each sound their timely rhapsodies.

The cloudy days and midnight moon,
The cooling breezes and monsoon
This gracious time with love festoon,
And banish all our old unease.

These rainy days delight provoke:
With saffron dyed my bridal cloak
The heavy showers sweetly soak—
Its borders flutter in the breeze.

45

آئے مست ڈہاڑے ساون دے
وہ ساون دے من بھاون دے

بدلے پورب ماڑ ڈکھن دے
کجلے بھورے سو سو ون دے
چارے طرفوں زور پون دے
سارے جوڑ وساون دے

چکویاں چکوے اغن پیہے
کوئل مور چچونے چیہے
سہنس چکور چنڈور پیہے
شاغل گیت سناون دے

ڈیہاں پینگھاں ساویاں پیلیاں
راتیں کھمنیاں کھمن رنگیلیاں
گج گج گاجاں کجن رسیلیاں
وقت سنگار سہاون دے

روہی راوے تھیاں گلزاراں
تھل چترانگ وی باغ بہاراں
گھنڈ توتاراں بارش باراں
چرچے دھاون گاون دے

چاندنی رات ملھاری ڈینگھ ہے
ٹھڈریاں ہیلاں رم جھم مینگھ ہے
سوہنی موسم لگڑا نینگھ ہے
گئے ویہلے غم کھاون دے

مد مستانی تے خوش دنڑے
سالھوں سوہے کیسر بھنڑے
سمجھوں مینگھ برساتوں سنڑے
جھڑ گے لانگھے لاون دے

These freshly fertile pastures see,
To which the cattle flock with glee:
My heart from all distress is free—
I burst in joy from my chemise!

وینجھ فرید آباد تھیوسے
مال مویشی شاد تھیوسے
دل دردوں آزاد تھیوسے
چولے انگ نہ ماون دے

46 Go Fetch Me Some Bracelets

Go fetch me some bracelets from far Jaisalmer—
A scarlet shawl too, which was dyed in Ajmer.

But let them be real and come straight from Marwar,
Not some copies, all twisted and queer.

Oh may he come quickly and not hang about—
To delay now what need is there here!

This shawl of affection, these bangles of love,
Both are signs of the Kak river's weir.

From Bikaner toe-rings I'll order myself,
On my right and my left foot to wear.

I'll put them on gladly to strut about in:
To my brother-in-law thanks will I bear.

Farid, if my lover will do what I say,
From my enemies what should I fear?

46

چوڑا انا ڈے جیسلمیر دا
سوہا رنگا ڈے خاص اجمیر دا

ہووے اصلی خاص مڑیچہ
نہ نقلی ول پھیر دا

جلدی آوے نا چر لاوے
کم نہیں اتھ دیر دا

برہوں دا چوڑا پریت دا سوہا
کاک ندی دے کھیر دا

بچھوا بیکانیری گھنساں
سجڑے کھیڑے پیر دا

سمجھوں پیساں پا ٹھمکیساں
تھورا چیساں ڈیر دا

یار فرید مینندم آکھیئے
کیا ہم پئے وے ویر دا

47 The Nomad-Maids

The sweet and slender nomad-maids
Out in desert stay.

By night they hunt for lovers' hearts:
They churn their pots by day.

What secret deadly darts they fire!
How many hearts they slay!

On those they sorely wound, alas,
No bandages they lay.

Their flocks of goats and cows and sheep
They drive with cries of 'hey!'

How many wretched passers-by
They ruthlessly waylay!

Like some fakir before his fire,
I've cast all pride away.

I lie before her door, since leashed
By love I may not stray.

Amidst my ever-growing woes
All joy is lost today.

47

وچ روہی دے رہندیاں
نازک نازو جٹیاں

راتیں کرن شکار دلیں دے
ڈینہاں ولوڑن مٹیاں

گجھڑے تیر چلاون کاری
سے سے دلڑیاں پھٹیاں

کر کر دردمنداں کوں زخمی
ہے ہے بدھن نہ پٹیاں

چھیڑن بھیڈاں بکریاں گائیں
لیلے گابے کٹیاں

کئی مسکین مسافر پھاتے
چور کتو نے ترٹیاں

دھوئیں دار فقیر تھیو سے
فخر وڈائیاں سٹیاں

ہیوں دلبر دے کتڑے در دے
برہوں پیاں گل گٹیاں

مونجھ فرید مزید ہمیشہ
اج کلھ خوشیاں گھٹیاں

48 Our Reservoir

Come, far above the Indus-stream
Let us sink our reservoir.

Up where the girls before their huts
Churn beneath the morning star.

Renowned in all the desert-hills
May its fame approach Marwar.

Let's—higher than Sukh Sagar's dunes—
Sink it on some lofty scar.

Let's dig it where the water flows:
Nothing should its clearness mar.

Let's choose a clear and level place
Where no brakes or thickets are.

Their camps may all the desert-folk
Strike, and journey from afar.

Let us be kind to Phullu Dha,
And make grateful Dina Lar.

Farid will live in desert-huts,
And forsake the town's bazaar.

48

ٹوبھ بنوا ڈے پکا تز تاڑ تے
سندھڑوں دور اتار تے

صبح سحوریں گھبکن ٹلیاں
جو ھیڑ دے اگواڑ تے

روہی راوے روہیں دھاں
ہوک پووے وچ ماڑ تے

اجڑے ٹبرے سکھ ساگھر دے
چڑھنا پووم پہاڑ تے

چو طرفوں ویہ پانی آوے
سوہنے صاف جھکاڑ تے

پاک ڈھر وچ ٹوبھا ماروں
نا جھت جھاڑ کجاڑ تے

روہی واس سمبھے لڈا وسن
اپنیاں جھوکاں ساڑ تے

کھلوڈھے تے منت لیسوں
تھورا چڑھیسوں دینے لاڑ تے

آن فرید سہیلیاں چنور ے
شہر بزار اجاڑ تے

49 Let's Build A Booth

Let's build a booth of desert-grass
Unrivalled in the pasturage.

I will not sit by pit or well
Or watercourse or field or hedge.

To see the desert-rains I'll leave
The Indus with my lineage.

Should water here run dry we'll go
Away to build a booth of sedge.

Without you I should loathe Bhambhor:
That you will stay have I your pledge?

Each bone of mine and all my flesh
Are smitten by love's steely edge.

49

جھوپڑ جوڑوں چک کھپ تھڈ تے
ایتھاں نہ ہووے سارے مڈ تے

نا وکڑے نا بند تے بہساں
نا گٹھ پار دی کھڈ تے

سانون آن سہمیساں روہی
سندھڑوں سگھری لڈ تے

جے پانی کھٹ ویسی بہسوں
ڈھائے تے کل اڈ تے

شہر بھنبور وی کھاون اوسم
ہوت نہ جاویں چھڈ تے

تیغ فرید برہوں دی وہ گئی
چم چم تے ہڈ ہڈ تے

50 The Pilu-Pickers

Come pick together, friends—
It's pilu harvest-day, oh!

See, some are white, green, yellow too,
And others brown or pale blue,
While some are red and mauve,
Vermilion or grey, oh!

The sands, now filled with heavenly fruit,
Destroy and burn our sorrow's root,
And all is spring: so come
And taste the fruit, I pray, oh!

Amidst the pilu-groves they throng,
Some bearing bags or baskets strong,
While some on heaps of fruit
Their hampers' contents lay, oh!

The pilu-trees are full of folk—
What scenes of rapture they evoke!
In shelters and in booths
A thousand others stay, oh!

The lovely maidens pick in rows
And from their beauty love's wind blows:
However cold the nights,
The breeze blows hot by day, oh!

The beauties wreak their deadly art:
Their eyebrows' blade and glances' dart
Are weapons swift and keen
Their lovers' hearts to slay, oh!

50

آ چنوں رل یار
پیلوں پکیاں نی وے

کئی بگڑیاں کئی ساویاں پیلیاں
کئی بھوریاں کئی پھکڑیاں نیلیاں
کئی اودیاں گلنار
کٹویاں رتیاں نی وے

بار تھئی ہے رشک ارم دی
سک سڑ گئی جڑھ ڈکھ تے غم دی
ہر جا باغ بہار
ساکھاں تکھیاں نی وے

پیلوں ڈیکھیاں دیاں گلزاراں
کہیں گل ٹوریاں کہیں سر کھاریاں
کئی لا بیٹھیاں بار
بھر بھر بچھیاں نی وے

جال جلوتیں تھئی آبادی
پل پل خوشیاں دم دم شادی
لوکی سہنس ہزار
کل تے پکھیاں نی وے

حوراں پریاں ٹولے ٹولے
حسن دیاں ہیلاں برہوں دے جھولے
راتیں ٹھڈیاں ٹھار
گوئکیں تتیاں نی وے

رکھدے ناز حسن پرور دے
ابرو تیغ تے تیر نظر دے
تیز تکھے ہتھیار
دلیاں پھٹیاں نی وے

Some give their fruit at par for grain,
While some take half as much again:
And some sell in the mart—
How carefully they weigh, oh!

Some keep on picking in the heat,
While others to the shade retreat:
And some outworn by toil
No further part do play, oh!

For their part they unleash their charms,
While here, like victims slain for alms,
Their lovers meekly wait—
How sweet is their display, oh!

Now, as they pick, upon some thorn
Their shawls and bodices are torn:
And so the womenfolk
With merry taunts inveigh, oh!

To pick the pilus did they come,
Until Farid-like they become
Unable to find ease
The victims of dismay, oh!

کئی ڈیون ان نال برابر
کئی گھن آون ڈیڈھے کر کر
کئی وچھن بازار
تلیاں تکیاں نی وے

کئی دھپ وچ چنڈیاں رہندیاں
کئی گھن چھاں چھویرے بہندیاں
کئی چن چن پیاں ہار
ہٹیاں تھیاں نی وے

ایڈوں عشوے غمزے نخرے
اوڈوں یار خرائتی بکرے
کسن کان تیار
رانداں رسیاں نی وے

پیلوں چندیں بوچھن لیراں
چولا وی تھیا لیر کتیراں
گلڑے کرن پچار
سینگیاں سکیاں نی وے

آیاں پیلوں چنن دے سانگے
اوڑک تھیاں فریدن وانگے
چھوڑ ارام قرار
ہکیاں بکیاں نی وے

Concordance

Numbers of poems in this selection, with the corresponding numbers in the standard editions of the *Diwan-e-Farid*.

1	43		26	205
2	137		27	17
3	4		28	36
4	73		29	33
5	247		30	15
6	139		31	209
7	76		32	241
8	200		33	69
9	37		34	230
10	178		35	169
11	170		36	47
12	150		37	116
13	63		38	151
14	154		39	42
15	32		40	31
16	9		41	224
17	240		42	192
18	221		43	117
19	244		44	183
20	95		45	175
21	252		46	6
22	82		47	136
23	130		48	197
24	194		49	202
25	163		50	167

Glossary

Aiman	The valley on the right of Mount Sinai where God spoke to Moses[A.S.]
Ajmer	A city in Rajasthan.
Baloch	The nomad-people to which Punnun belonged.
Bhambhor	The city in Sind of which Sassi's father was king.
Bikaner	Capital of a former princely state of Marwar.
Bistami	The ecstatic Sufi Abu Yazid Bistami (d. 874).
Dina Lar	Dessert-girl of the Lar tribe whom Khwaja Farid married, and who is addressed in several poems.
Fakhr ud-Din	Elder brother and pir of Khwaja Farid also known as Khwaja Fakhr-e-Jahan (d. 1871).
Haram Mai Hotan	The desert-girl of the Lar tribe whom Khwaja Farid married, and who is addressed in several of his poems.
Hir	The daughter of the Sial chieftain of Jhang who loved Ranjha, but was married to Khera against her will.
Hot	The tribal name of Punnun.
Ibn ul Arabi	The famous Spanish Sufi (d.1240), who gave the doctrine of mystical monism its classic formulation.
Jaisalmer	Capital of a former princely state in Marwar
Joseph	The Prophet, whose matchless beauty is often cited in conventional poetic conceit.
Kak	Dessert river associated with the legend of Mumal.
Kech	The area of Balochistan ruled by Punnun's father.
Khera	The tribe to which Hir's husband belonged.
Khwaja Nur-Muhammad	A well-known Sufi teacher of Mahar in Bahawalpur, also known as Khwaja Qibla-e-Alam (d. 1791), who was the spiritual ancestor of Khwaja Farid, being the pir of his great-grand father.

Laila	The daughter of an Arab chieftain, followed wherever she went by Majnun, who loved her to distraction and was ever hoping for a glimpse of her.
Mahar	The town in eastern Bahawalpur where Khwaja Nur Muhammad lived and is buried.
Mahinwal	The name given to Sohni's lover, after he had become a herds man for her sake.
Majnun	The title given to Qais, the lover of Laila, because of the madness which his love brought him.
Malhir	A place in lower Sindh, sometimes used as the equivalent of Kech.
Mansur	The famous Sufi Mansur Hallaj (d. 922), executed in Baghdad on a charge of heresy.
Maru	Name of the dessert through which Sassi wandered in search of Punnun.
Marwar	The desert-country occupying the wet of Rajasthan, immediately to the east of Bahawalpur.
Mumal	The Rajput princess who loved Rano.
Phullu Dha	Local desert-chieftain who used to entertain Khwaja Farid.
Pilu	Berry-like fruit of the jal-tree.
Punnal	Affectionate form of Punnun.
Punnun	The son of Baloch ruler of Kech, who loved Sassi and came to be with her in Bhambhor, but was abducted by his kinsmen while Sassi slept; also addressed as Baloch, Hot, and Punnal.
Ranjha	The lover of Hir, whom she got her father to employ as a herds man, who later became a yogi in order to revisit her after her marriage.
Rano	The lover of Mumal.
Sadiq Khan	Sadiq Muhammad Khan IV, ruler of Bahawalpur state (1866-1899), who assumed power on attaining his majority on 1879 after a lengthy British regency, and was well known for his devotion to Khwaja Farid.

Saifal	The her of a tale from the *Arabian Nights*, retold in Siraiki verse by Lutf Ali (1781), which tells of his adventurous quest for his beloved, the fairy princess Badi ul Jamal.
Sassi	The daughter of the king of Bhambhor who loved the Baloch prince Punnun: after Punnun had been stolen away by his kins men while she slept, she embarked on a hopeless pursuit of him across the burning sands of the Maru Thal, there at last to die.
Savan	The month July-August, when the rains of the monsoon come.
Sial	The tribe to which Hir belonged.
Sohni	The daughter of a potter of Gujrat, who used to cross the river Chenab on a water-pot to visit her lover Mahinwal.
Sukh Sagar	A desert-pool which Khwaja Farid used to visit.
Sumal	The sister of Mumal, who was one night dressed as a man to lie with Mumal in order to incite her lover Rano's jealousy.
Thal	The Maru dessert, scene of Sassi's torments.
Tur	Mount Sinai, where Moses[A.S.] was granted his vision of God.
Yazid	The Umayyad Caliph (d. 683) considered by the Shias to be responsible for the massacre of Hussain and his followers at the battle of Karbala, annually commemorated in the mourning-ceremonies of Muharram.

Khwaja Farid's Family and Spiritual Lineage

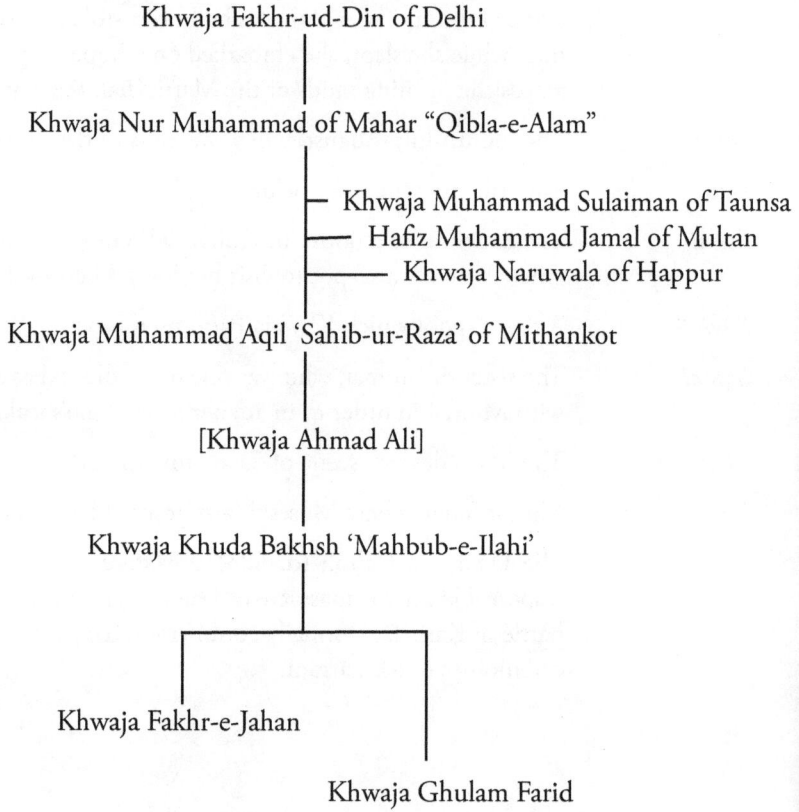

Khwaja Fakhr-ud-Din of Delhi

Khwaja Nur Muhammad of Mahar "Qibla-e-Alam"

— Khwaja Muhammad Sulaiman of Taunsa
— Hafiz Muhammad Jamal of Multan
— Khwaja Naruwala of Happur

Khwaja Muhammad Aqil 'Sahib-ur-Raza' of Mithankot

[Khwaja Ahmad Ali]

Khwaja Khuda Bakhsh 'Mahbub-e-Ilahi'

Khwaja Fakhr-e-Jahan

Khwaja Ghulam Farid

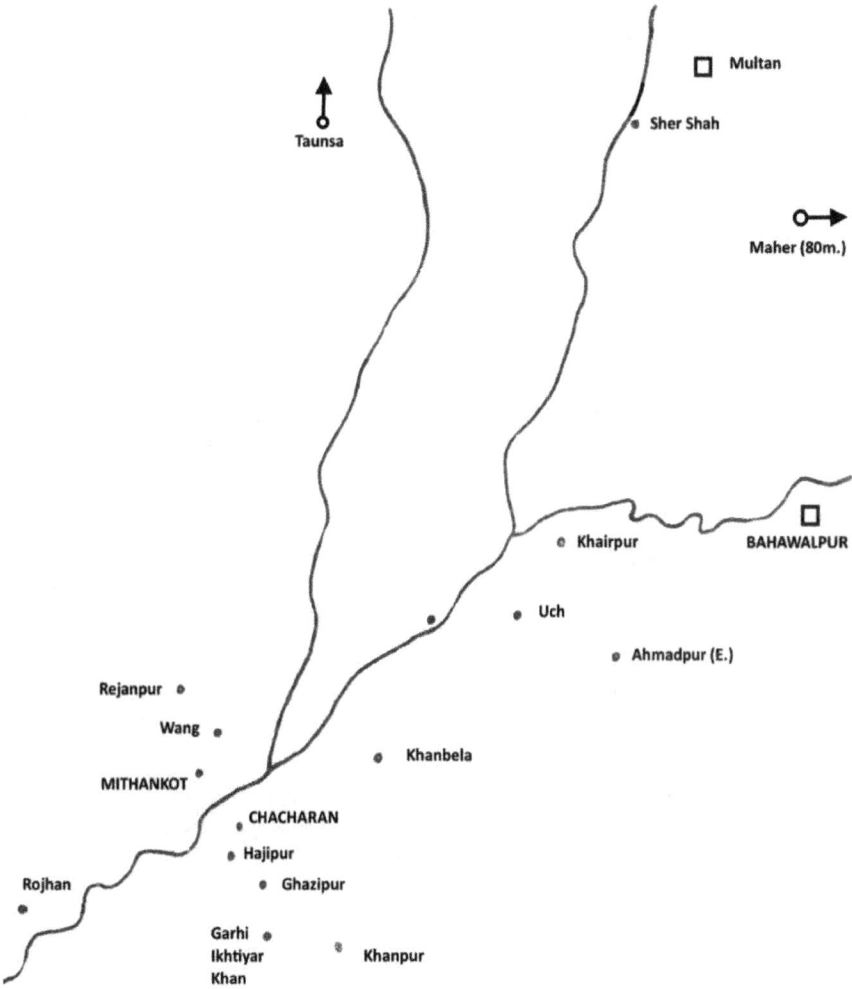

MAP
Showing some of the places
mentioned in the text

Index of Names

All personal names mentioned in the text are included here, except for those of the Prophets, and the early leaders of Islam, down to the Caliph Ali. The numbers refer to the Lesson in which the name is mentioned.